HOW NOT
TO KILL
YOUR
PLANTS

HOW NOT TO KILL YOUR PLANTS

NIK SOUTHERN

HODDER &
STOUGHTON

Contents

IN
PLANTS
WE
TRUST

As a kid growing up on a council estate who found solace when visiting her grandparents' plant-filled home, I've always understood the power of nature to transform. So when I started my floristry business, Grace & Thorn, my philosophy was simple: to help people bring plants and flowers into their lives – however concrete their space may be.

As more and more people cram into cities, space is becoming sacred. The houses we buy are smaller, landlords prevent us from personalising our properties – and owning a garden... who does? But, as a result, we're reclaiming the space around us as our own urban jungles. Throughout London, I see nature tumbling over balconies, lining up on windowsills and blocking up walkways. And within these walls, inside our homes, nature is taking over, too. Greening up your gaff is an easy, inexpensive and landlord-friendly way to style your home, breathing life into it without having to do much at all.

Indoors or outdoors, dressing a space with plants and flowers has never been so mood-shakingly exciting. Not only does it give us a feeling of instant style gratification but it is the gift that keeps on giving – we can watch them grow like our very own children. And if we look after plants, they will look after us, improving our health, happiness and homes (see page 151 for more on their endless benefits). No wonder everyone wants a piece of plant ass!

It's impossible to scroll through Instagram without realising that plants are having an 'it' moment, but I do hate the idea of nature being in fashion. I wrote this book to be a plant bible for anyone who wants to green up their home – or 'gaff' as we like to call it. Whether you're green-fingered or not this book will help you understand your plants' needs in order to understand where to place them: bathrooms can become fern-filled rainforests and sunny windowsills home to desert-dwelling cacti.

I want this book to open your eyes to plant possibilities everywhere, to help you remember your plant names and learn not to overwater! But before we get started, let's get one thing straight: I am not a botanist nor a horticultural expert. Everything I know, I know by doing. I've run my florist for five years and have learnt a few things along the way. I get that many people are overwhelmed by plants, so I'm taking everything back to the roots – Odyssey-style. This book isn't meant to sit on your coffee table; I want you to take it with you on the Tube or the bus. Use it, water it and may soil fall from between the pages.

GOING BACK
TO MY ROOTS

I feel like a fish out of water when I am in a room without flowers or plants. I almost struggle to breathe. Luckily, so many people are riding the botanical wave right now that I am very rarely found in that situation.

I constantly seek out plants and flowers wherever I go, looking out for the different ways they have been displayed and arranged. Hosts will find me rude as my eyes flit around the place, looking for what green goodies they have hidden on shelves and tucked into corners. Plants and flowers bring life into a room. Plants are like the steady family that are always there, while flowers are the flighty, flirty friends that add that touch of vibrancy and fun to every party they attend.

I love how more and more florists are defying traditions and arranging flowers in the most beautiful, natural way. But don't get me wrong, it's not always been so pretty. Even after the original rock 'n' roll florist, Constance Spry (we'll meet her later), shook the petals off the traditional twentieth century, flowers fell into a rut again. Think garage flowers all struggling to breath in luminous green cellophane and hideous netting. People fell out of love with them because they were being poorly presented. I was one of them. Before I started Grace & Thorn, I hardly ever bought flowers for myself. I used to feel intimidated walking into a florist and, if I'm honest, pretty uninspired. It was always the same old flowers, same old cellophane and the same old colour combinations.

I fell in love with nature in the back garden, behind the bike shed.

Inner-city London wasn't where my love for nature was nurtured. My mum and dad never had green fingers and our gaff certainly never had a plant in it (until I opened my shop that is). It was during regular trips to my nonna and grandpa's house in leafy north London where my love affair with flowers and plants began.

My nonna and grandpa were originally from Puglia, in the south of Italy, and their house was my sanctuary. Being the eldest of four, with working parents, I had to grow up pretty quickly. My nonna and grandpa's home was a respite from my otherwise grey, urban childhood.

Going there was like opening the door to the Emerald City of Oz or making my way through the wardrobe to Narnia. I found paradise and excitement around every corner. Imposing and grand to a child, their Victorian home in an ordinary London suburb had countless eccentricities: from the grandparents in it to the ornate vintage Italian-style bar that housed

rows of dusty old spirit bottles. And it was that passionate Italian blood running through my nonna's veins that nurtured the mini Kew Gardens that swept through the entirety of the house and into the back yard.

Their garden was full of rambling roses, grape vines, runner beans and tomatoes, and their house, well, that was almost as green as the outside. Massive cheese plants propped up with bamboo took over the living room, spotted begonia plants, lemons and scented geraniums dominated the windowsills and the tops of the cupboards – every corner of their house was

crammed with plants. They used to get me working for them, too: weeding, crushing grapes in an old barrel for their homemade wine with my bare toes and picking my first real tomatoes ready to place on top of our homemade pizzas!

I vividly remember reading the book *The Secret Garden* when I was in primary school. Plonked in the middle of built-up Islington, north London, our playground had a huge locked wooden door on one side that only the caretaker could enter. Crowds of children would press their small faces up to it, trying to peek through the gaps and spy the magical walled garden beyond. Looking back now, it was probably just somewhere the teachers could sneak a fag on their lunch break, but at the time, the garden was a wonder to me: crumbling, overgrown and, at times, quite sinister. Something about it gave me a sense of intrigue and peace.

Never really a natural academic, I found it hard to concentrate at school. My mind was always wandering and my schoolbooks were covered in doodles of trees and flowers. It was the walk to primary school that I loved the most. Walking through Camden Passage in Angel with its shops filled to the brim with antiquities and curiosities, we used to cut through, down along the canal, which was idyllic on a spring day – a far cry from the harsh concrete exterior of the building I lived in. I also loved going to our local park, Victoria Park (or Vicky Park as it's known affectionately to locals). Vicky Park has always been a haven for the working classes of East London, right back to the Victorian times, when this may have been the only bit of greenery an East End kid would ever encounter. Even when I was a child, it was a huge treat for us to go – my parents were quite strict and we were never allowed to go on our own.

Vicky Park has a massive pond and I remember loving the huge weeping willows we stood under while we fed the ducks. Back then there was no posh coffee shop like now, but the park was a magical place for a city child, and proof that nature did actually exist! My nonna and

I would collect caterpillars and keep them in empty coffee pots with lettuce leaves. I can't remember what happened to them, poor things, but I always remember that nature made me really happy.

When I was 14 we moved to Enfield, another leafy suburb on the outskirts of London. I DIED AND WENT TO HEAVEN. We moved to a bloody tiny house for how many of us there were: two parents, four kids and THREE bedrooms! BUT we had a 100-foot garden. Bliss. It was in this garden that I found peace and solace from three younger siblings and an Irish and Italian mum and dad! While my brother and sisters were out playing with friends, I was playing with plants and flowers in the garden.

SO... to cut a long story short, what did a child from a concrete council estate do with all this love for nature? I got a job in recruitment, where I stayed for 13 years.

During that time, I married, moved to Surrey and finally had a garden of my own. Instead of bumping into me at parties, I was tending to plants in the garden. My garden became my obsession. Fast-forward eight years, I got a divorce and moved back to London. Moving to Canary Wharf – aka Skyscraper City – I couldn't have been more miserable. From country living to this? I missed my fields, woodlands and garden. I headed back to my home turf of Islington but after a year of living in a flat without any outside space, I moved into my sister's dreary basement flat just so I could have a garden again! YES! Sod the damp, I had some green back in my life! It was the start of a new chapter, but I still felt like I was missing something. I just couldn't put my finger on it...

I drifted from one recruitment job to the next and this wasn't like me at all – I was Steady Eddie: stable and reliable. In one year I found myself at three different companies and I realised that no matter where I was, I just hated it. I was at a loss. I was done with recruitment but as far as I was concerned I didn't have any other skills – I left school at 18! Feeling totally lost and not sure where my life was heading, I called up a business coach I knew from my first company. After much consoling, he suggested I try the Myers Briggs Humanmetrics Test. The test asks you LOADS of questions and then it analyses your answers to work out your personality type. Sound too good to be true? Well, it got mine down to a T! I quickly looked up the suggested careers for my personality and three jumped out at me. The first was interior designer. I LOVED interiors and was forever changing my home around and scouring vintage shops and eBay for bits and pieces to fill it with, so I signed up for an evening class. This started and finished very quickly, as there was just too much theory work involved. The second was gardener. I obviously loved gardening, but it was the third one that caught my imagination: florist!

I signed up to the best course I could get into and I knew from day one that this was what I wanted to do. I went to bed dreaming of flowers and woke up thinking of them. But I struggled with the traditional teaching – we were told to keep our bouquets rounded like a 'pregnant belly' and I just couldn't do it! I loved the flowers but hated the formal ways they were displayed. My instinct was to let them be free! My teachers despaired. But despite that, I felt that I had finally, at the age of 34, found my calling. After I completed my course, I did a couple of work experience stints but soon got bored with sweeping floors and stripping stems. I kept being told there were no jobs out there, and certainly nothing for someone with zero experience. So what did I do?! I shit myself and went back to recruitment, didn't I?!

But I couldn't stop thinking about flowers. I practised making floral displays in my living room, read endless books and watched hours of YouTube videos. I knew it was what I needed to do, but I just didn't know *how*. When my boss pulled me into the office one day and said, 'Your head's not in this, is it?', I quit. 'No', I responded, 'I think it's best I go!' And so I did. For the next six months I was unemployed, spending my days moping around watching *Gossip Girl* and smoking rollies.

I used to frequent the Bricklayers Arms in Shoreditch quite a bit as that's where my sister and her fashion mates used to hang out. When I say 'frequent', I would turn up and basically try and convince them all that they needed my flowers in their lives! A couple of them felt sorry for me and gave me a shot. YESSSS!

I didn't make any money at first because I would buy the flowers to do a practice run and then buy them all again for the real deal! I used to, and still do, always worry that the person receiving what I'd done won't like it... it drives me insane but that's what pushes me to do the best job I can. Always. I soon started getting orders from my mates and when Valentine's Day came round I managed to get out 20 bouquets without a hitch! The flat was full of flowers and I drove my poor flatmates insane, but seeing my Facebook feed full of pics of *my* flowers gave me such a buzz! I wanted MORE!

Then I got really lucky. One of my friends who was then head of PR for Whistles asked me to come up with an arrangement (four little jam jars full of flowers in a wooden crate, called The Pandora's Box, and still our best-selling product!) to send to all the top editors in London. My other mate worked at *The Sunday Times Style* magazine, so I called her and said, 'My flowers are on the way to your office! BIG THEM UP FOR ME!'. She called me and said they were already on the editor's mood board. After that, *Style* did a feature on florists and there I was... on a three-page spread with the UK's best florists! My inbox that Monday morning was full! One email from L.K. Bennett asked if I wanted to do their annual Chelsea in Bloom competition. What? I didn't even know what that was! I hadn't even done a wedding at that point! I remember telling my mate and him saying, 'Bloody Hell, Nik, this is like an episode of *Faking It*. Can you pull this off?'.

OF COURSE I COULD!

I managed to find myself a small windowless basement studio (what was it with me and basements?) in Dalston and with my friends and boyfriend by my side we installed six windows and went on to win the People's Choice Award.

Soon I needed to look for a larger studio space and that's when I found my beloved shop on Hackney Road. The rest is history, as they say. A history full of tears, exhaustion, love, laughter, fall-outs, sleepless nights, self-doubt and joy, BUT, most of all, I was alive again... I was living and breathing what I loved to do. I now knew what was missing that I could never put my finger on before: nature.

HOW TO USE THIS BOOK

Before we get started, let's get one thing out in the open: everyone kills plants. Me, probably Monty, and most definitely your mate with green fingers. There, I said it. My advice? Don't be a fusspot. Did you know, one of the easiest ways to kill a plant is overwatering it? Put that watering can down! To keep your plant alive, you have to understand where your plant has come from – you have to go back to its roots. Think about it this way: plants have evolved over thousands of years to adapt to specific conditions, be it succulents storing water in the dry desert or ferns needing less light under the damp canopy of the Amazonian rainforest. Sure, you might not be able to put Tarzan up for the night, but your house already presents you with many microclimates that recreate the natural wonders of the world. From a hot, south-facing windowsill, to the top of a kitchen cupboard that gets all the steam from your kettle, you just have to think a little differently about your space. And the same goes for what you give your plant. If it only rains twice a year in the desert, does your cacti want all that water? If a fern has evolved on the forest floor, why have you left it scorching on your unshaded sill? Once you understand these principles, may you all live happily ever after.

This book is designed to teach you everything you need to green up your gaff, Grace & Thorn-style. From the plants to the pots and everything in between, it's time to roll up your sleeves and get your hands dirty. I understand that walking into a florist can be a bit mind-boggling, so see this as your private tour. I'm going to guide you through the palms and petals out into the hot, dry desert where we can observe the cacti. We'll hang out with cheese plants under the canopies of the rainforest, and stop off for a glass of Italian rosé and sniff the scented geraniums on the way! To help you find your bearings, I've split stuff into sections. Start from the beginning, middle or end. No Google Maps required.

1

Chapter 1: Back to the roots
Whenever someone comes to me with a plant problem, the first thing I tell them to do is to go back to the roots, back to where the plant has come from, to understand what it needs. In this first section you will learn the types of environments your favourite houseplants come from, then we'll look at where these environments might exist in your home. With this knowledge, you'll know what plants will thrive in your gaff and the perfect place to put them. Simple.

2

Chapter 2: Starting a plant family
Now we've learnt what plants will be happy in our gaff, it's time to green it up! See this as the plant parents' starter pack. From where to go plant shopping to making the perfect purchase to finding your botanical BFF. I am also keen to get you to see plants differently, as one man's plant trash may be another man's plant treasure. We'll also be looking at our four-legged friends and finding out how to make harmony in the home.

Chapter 3: Pot luck

OK, I confess, at Grace & Thorn, we're all pot-heads! We spend hours sourcing the perfect pots, from ceramics to copper and we even paint our own, too. You'll learn all you need to know to repot your plants and how to style and arrange them, à la Grace & Thorn. Learn how to help your tiny plant babies shine and let the big ones graduate to show-off school. Be prepared to up the style ante with green, green and more green.

Chapter 4: How not to kill your plants

Here we learn how to make your plant babies strong, healthy and really, really good-looking! I mostly get asked the same plant questions all the time, so I decided to put all the relevant info together in one place. We'll check into a Houseplant Hospital and even perform divine intervention by bringing dying plants back to life. Amen.

Chapter 5: Free your flowers

Palms and petals. Flowers and foliage. At Grace & Thorn the two go hand in hand. We're obsessed with all things green, and while we concentrate on houseplants in this book, flowers are also a BIG part of our story. Instead of giving you all the deets on flower arranging (that would take a whole other book), we'll look at the basics of the bouquet, from our fave florals and foliage, to creating a hand-tied display. Expect a few floristry rules to be broken.

Chapter 6: Plant porn

Plant directories are so overwhelming. In the Grace & Thorn Plant Encyclopaedia (aka Plant porn), instead of listing every plant out there, I've just included my absolute faves and their key rules for care. Even better: all the plants in this book are on the low-maintenance side of the scale. You're welcome.

A potted history: history of the houseplant

Whether it's for their fragrance, style or to make a banging G&T, people have been bringing plants into their homes for thousands of years. And even before homes were invented, ferns hung out with dinosaurs in their gaff: the planet! The history of the houseplant is wicked – from female pioneers growing gardens upside down to sailors risking their lives to bring citrus trees back across the oceans. We give a knowing nod to the Victorians trying to combat pollution with the humble fern, and then have our minds blown as a houseplant reference book becomes the second biggest seller after the Bible. But throughout all this, one thing holds true: over thousands of years we've all been plant obsessed. You, me, your great-great-great-great nan – oh, and T-Rex.

No one actually knows when the first plant was brought inside, but the first recorded examples can be found in artworks from Ancient Greece. The Greeks decorated almost every part of their lives, from their streets to the insides of their homes, so it's no wonder that they turned their attention to plants. Ancient Egyptian records indicate the first official trade of flora between countries, and the badass Egyptian Queen Hatshepsut grew frankincense in her temple in 1478 BC. In ancient China, the Chinese pimped their homes with plants to signify their wealth, and Roman villas were scented with the blossom of citrus trees. In around 600 BC, King Nebuchadnezzar built botanical bliss down by the rivers of Babylon. He made the gardens for his wife, Queen Amytis, who missed the green hills of home, filling them with fragrant blooms – every plant you can imagine and trees hanging from the ceiling!

In the seventeenth century, the gap year was invented by adventurers who left their homes to explore the world. Plant discoveries from far and wide were brought back by blustering sea captains, who often did a little macramé on the side! Sir Walter Raleigh returned with the humble tomato plant and is claimed to have introduced Britain to the orange by returning with pips from the unknown citrus fruit. Many plants were lost at sea or did not survive their new climates, but the fruits of those plants that did make it allowed for great experimentations into how to keep these tropical species alive in our cooler temperatures.

Houseplants got their first shout out in *The Garden of Eden*, a MASSIVE book written by Sir Platt in 1652. He wrote of 'cultivating plants indoors'. Over three hundred years ago, the first book aimed at the 'city gardener' (sound familiar?) remarked on how fellow citizens indulged their love for gardening in the little space the city offered by, 'furnishing their rooms or chambers with basins of flowers and bough pots'. Pots were a big deal in the eighteenth century, when they started to be mass-produced for commercial uses. Leading the charge was Mr 'mum's favourite dinner plate' Wedgwood, who saw opportunities in the expanding craze for keeping plants indoors. He wrote that the perfect pot 'stands firm but not look heavy... to hold a good quantity of flowers... to be different earth, colour or composition, from the common earthenware of the time... and to come at a moderate price'. High five, Mr Wedgwood! We have a lot is common, especially when it comes to his Hedgehog

pots. Let's call them ancestors of the animal heads we have in the G&T shop, except that in his pots you could plant the seeds to bloom like the hedgehog spikes. Neat.

If I could travel back in time, it would be to the Victorian era. This is probably because those years were a BIG deal for houseplants. As a result of the pollution created by the industrial revolution, plants really suffered. Along came Mr Warde, who developed the Wardian case – which you and I know as a terrarium – to look after his ferns. This glass case also provided perfect protection for plants transported from across the seas, and so a whole new world of plant possibilities opened up as a consequence. (See pages 61–63 for more on terrariums and how to make your own.) Thanks to the Wardian case, Grace & Thorn's local borough of Hackney was once home to one of the largest hot-houses in the world! Conrad Loddiges had come to the suburban village (ho ho) of Hackney to become a gardener. He started a small seed business, writing to people all over the world, asking them to send him seeds they had collected from wilder climates. As his collection grew, he was responsible for introducing both rhubarb and rhododendron into Britain. Nice one, Conrad. Loddiges' was one of the first nurseries to see the potential in the Wardian Case – on a much grander scale – and their notoriety blossomed. Like us at Grace & Thorn, Loddiges believed that the best way to look after a plant is to understand where it has come from. Loddiges created a revolutionary heating system that mimicked the conditions of a tropical rainforest. With banana trees as tall as the ceiling and 'magical inside rainfall', visiting Londoners were amazed by the heady jungle located just off Mare Street in East London. Due to rising property values in the growing 'village' of

Hackney (also sound familiar?), Conrad's son found it increasingly difficult to negotiate a new lease from the landowner and, alongside the growing pollution in London affecting the plants, Loddiges closed his doors. Still today, Hackney hosts two massive palm trees outside the town hall. Ever wondered how they got there? Well, now you know.

The nineteenth century saw advances in the home and as domestic heating improved, plants moved from hot-houses to conservatories and into our living rooms. The arrival of the sash window from Holland led to the design of windowsills and balconies and houseplants flourished, natch.

The twentieth century started a snobbishness when it came to having flowers in the home. One social rule maintained that if you mixed up your floral arrangements, it suggested that your garden was too small to grow enough of one variety. Pfft.

One lady then shook all the petals off what had become a petty, dull industry. Her name was Constance Spry, the Fairy Godmother of the anarchic florist. When everyone else was cramming identical flowers into tight vases, Spry was creating all-foliage bouquets, adding vegetables, berries and other non-traditional elements. She'd rummage around in the cupboards of her clients and bring out unusual and outrageous objects to be used as vases. Constance caused controversy even after her death: the announcement of an exhibition of her work at The Design Museum caused the two museum's founders to threaten resignation, claiming flowing arranging was 'styling' not 'design'. Say, what? Constance, we salute you!

The modernisation of the 1950s meant that what families gained in up-to-date, modern housing, they lost in precious green space. Homes were now flats and, as people looked for ways to make their flats more appealing, the humble houseplant became No. 1 in every how-to home magazine. The introduction of Scandinavian design, after the war, had an obvious impact, as people wanted clean and fresh-looking homes – something plants can offer in the pot load. This craze carried on well into the '60s, when a Dr. Hessayon published the ultimate houseplant book, *Be Your Own House Plant Expert*. Astonishingly, it was claimed to be the biggest-selling reference book after the Bible! But by the end of the twentieth century things had started to go stale. Younger women, especially, started to see plants as a burden – another thing to look after on top of everything else.

The 1980s saw houseplants considered as design features. They complemented the wooden and chrome style of modern houses and, let's face it, no self-respecting person with a GIANT Nokia could be without a giant cheese plant, too. There had been a strange stigma that houseplants were bad for you because they might attract pests and dust into the home, but when NASA launched their research that having plants in the home was absolutely beneficial for your health, plants flew off the shelves. Unsurprisingly, many of our parents' generation look back at this time and cringe. Not just at their bouffant hair, but at their houseplants too!

In the '00s plants lost their cool again because everyone associated them with their geography teacher and dental surgeries.

Luckily for us, in recent years, plants have made (another) comeback. I do hate the idea of nature being in vogue but it's impossible not to scroll through Instagram, walk into a coffee shop or sit in a train station and not eye-spy something green. Phew! But we can look back to history to see why plants are relevant now. Like the Greeks, we are all looking for more ways of self-expression, like the Victorians we are trying to combat pollution, and like anyone living anywhere in the modern world we are trying to reclaim nature, in whatever mini-succulent-sized way we can.

Plants in places

It's New Years' Eve 2015 and my partner and I are sitting in the Indian Embassy, in London, waiting to get our visas for our flight that leaves in a few hours (last-minute, I know!). Looking around the lonely waiting room at the few token houseplants, I was struck by two emotions:
1. Nurture. I wanted to go and sort them out immediately! Pot them up properly, water them and tend to their poor brown leaves.
2. Happiness. These plants are at home here, and I love that!
That moment inspired this series of photographs. I love the places where plants have been knocking about for years – think doctors' surgeries, minicab offices, the dry cleaners and the restaurant down the road. Anyone who takes the time to look after their plants, in between performing root canals, is a great person in my eyes. These are the unsung plant heroes who hold down jobs while propping up their palms. Their reward? A happy plant family. A special shout out goes to the lead in the film, *Leon!* If an assassin can find time to care for his calathea, there is hope for us all.

I like a man who is enthusiastic, and watching Monty's great big grin when he talks about gardening does it for me. And he has dogs. What's not to love? Friday night is all about having a big glass of red with Monty. I get home, get my whippets on the sofa and *Gardener's World* on the telly. The other day, Monty pulled some carrots out of the ground and called them pathetic. Can you imagine Titchmarsh saying that? I can relate: gardening does not have to be perfect, but Monty, you're not far off.

BACK TO **1** THE ROOTS

WHY ARE MY SUCCULENTS STRUGGLING IN MY BASEMENT FLAT?

It's questions like this from my customers, friends and mum that made me want to write this book. My advice is simple: emulate the environment your plant hails from and it will be a happy chappy (save your dark basement for shade-lovin' rainforest plants, see pages 46–53).

All the plants you know and love have evolved over thousands of years to adapt to their environments: cacti survived desert predators by growing huge 'don't f&^k with me' spikes – and have you ever wondered why your cheese plants grows those funny air roots? These helped them climb off the dark rainforest floor and up into the light! Nearly all our favourite houseplants have come from hot spots all over the world: from the dry desert to the wet, steamy undergrowth of the rainforest. Luckily for us, the wonders of the modern home mean that these tropical treasures can come and live with us, but we need to understand where they have come from originally so that we know where to place them in our homes, so that we can all, ultimately, live happily ever after.

When I came to write this book, rather than doing a room-by-room guide, I wanted to make something much more practical – and realistic. The two-up-two-down approach just isn't relevant to the modern indoor gardener living in shared flats, warehouses, basements, boats and sometimes even a cupboard (that'll cost you £600 a month if you're in London). When you're squished for space, sometimes kitchens come without sinks and bathrooms without showers. So, instead, I wanted to think about the different climates – and microclimates – your home has, and what plants will thrive in them. We can find plant potential in every type of room and the small forgotten spaces, too – that spot above the kettle that gets lovely and humid or an unused corner that catches the afternoon sun. Rooms are interchangeable, heaters come on in the winter, windows swing open on sunny days, so let's discover the different climates our favourite houseplants come from originally, and then we'll have a look at where those climates exist in your home, wherever and whatever that may be.

RAINFOREST

Rainforest canopy plants
* Palms
* Cheese plants
* Philodendrons
* Devil's ivy

Rainforest floor plants
* Ferns
* Begonia
* Fittonia
* Maranthus
  'Prayer Plant'

To understand rainforest plants, we need to understand the climate of the rainforest. Sure, there is a clue in the name – it can get more than 2.5m of rain every year, and many rainforest plants have adapted by growing leaves with a waxy coating to help water to roll off of them. But that level of rain changes as you get further into the undergrowth. The easiest way to look at it is by splitting the rainforest into layers and then at the different types of houseplants that come from each one.

At the very top, trees grow close together making up the canopy layer that blocks out direct sunlight. Below them, vines weave up through the trees creating a green blanket that protects the plants below from rain, wind and extreme heat; it also holds in warmth at night. Because the air doesn't escape easily through the tree canopy, the humidity underneath is extremely high. Some plants on the rainforest floor have evolved to grow aerial roots, which they use to attach themselves to other trees to climb up towards the light. So, when it comes to thinking about where these plants can live in your home, you need to think of places with enough room for them to show off. OK, so they're not quite swinging off vines like Tarzan, but the jungle likes to get massive! On the shaded forest floor, there's no direct light and the soil is damp – the soil in a rainforest is made up of leaves, wood, compost and loads of animal poop! You must give your plants good drainage to allow the roots to grow freely without finding wet patches where they will rot.

So what have we learnt?
Overall, rainforest plants like indirect sun and so tolerate low-light locations well. However, the level of light depends on the layer of the rainforest from which they originate. Palm trees, at the top, love exposed sun, whereas ferns from the forest floor like it less bright. Climbers, like the cheese plant, can survive with low light levels but have evolved to seek out sun, so make sure they get enough. Humidity lower down is high so keep that mister at hand. They also like to stay damp, so try not to let the soil dry out but you should be watering your rainforest plants, not soaking them. They don't like extreme heat, so keep away from radiators.

Rainforest gaffs
- Lovely steamy bathrooms for humidity lovers
- Bright sitting rooms with space for climbers to seek sun
- The dark downstairs loo where shade lovers can thrive
- Walls for climbing vines to grow
- Near the kettle will keep tropical plants nice and humid

WHAT THE FERN!?

Boston fern
Nephrolepis exaltata

Rating
Needy flatmate.

Name check
Think shade, think *FernGully*.

My top five ferns
- Boston fern (*Nephrolepis exaltata*)
- Maidenhair fern (*Adiantum*)
- Staghorn fern (*Platycerium*)
- Venus hair fern
  (*Adiantum capillus-veneris*)
- Asparagus fern (*I know, it doesn't count, but I love it. Also see Subtropics, page 64*)

The deets
Ferns are over 300 million years old, but they're still one of the freshest plants around. They not only hung out with dinosaurs but these asexual plants could fly the flag for LGBTQ plant rights. Ferns can be quite bashful when you take them home and they don't like neglect. Just think of how damp and shady the rainforest floor is – these guys are in shock! But given the right love and attention, they can turn out big, bushy and beautiful. There are almost 2,000 species, but we get heart eyes for the Boston and maidenhair ferns.

Back to the roots
Most ferns grow on the shady forest floor where the sunlight is filtered by all the plants above, so never place your fern in direct sunlight as it will burn. All that vegetation above means it's really humid down there so spritz regularly to keep them moist. Also, remember that radiators dry out the air, so either move your fern or mist, mist, mist! The damp floor means you should never let your fern dry out but this doesn't mean constant watering, as it'll end up with a soggy bottom. My advice is just to keep a strict eye on it and use the finger test (see page 202). Ferns need feeding little and often and can go weak if left without nutrients. If your fern is in among other plants, make sure to give it some space: its fronds need room to grow, and snip off any dead fronds to allow new ones to flourish.

How not to kill your fern
The most common problems are yellowing leaves and brown tips. This means the air is too dry. Turn the humidity up by misting regularly. If the leaves are pale or you notice scorch marks, it's getting sunburnt – move it somewhere out of the glare. If a line of brown dots appears on the underside of the leaf, don't panic, these are spore cases that can be used to grow new plants. If, however, you see brown cases scattered all over the leaves this could be pest scale and it's time to check it into the houseplant hospital (see page 208).

HIGH FLYER

Philodendron
Philodendron scandens

Rating
Pretty and indestructible.

Name check
Time to brush up on your Latin: the name comes from Greek words *philo* meaning love and affection, and *dendron* meaning tree.

The deets
This humble houseplant may be overlooked, as it hangs around in the home of most houseplant lovers. But behind the scenes, its beautiful decorative leaves have inspired some of the world's most respected artists from Eames to Erdem. Its rise to fame began in the nineteenth century when botanist Heinrich Wilhelm Schott identified 587 species of philodendron on an expedition to Brazil and brought some home to the Imperial Garden of Vienna. This plant is one of my faves, as it is great for making your jungle massive – you can pin it across walls, drape it around picture frames or hang it from macramé. But, we need to go back to the start of the story to understand it.

Back to the roots
The first clue is in the name – a tree lover! The species of philodendron most commonly used as a houseplant is the climber, which started life on the rainforest floor of the Latin Americas and used its roots to climb up towards the light. They start with small leaves and, as they grow up a tree, their leaves will get bigger to get more sun. But remember, the top is still obscured by a canopy of trees. Therefore, these guys grow well in both shaded and bright places but avoid direct light as they will scorch! During the rainy season in the wild – for more than half the year – they will often experience rain on a daily basis, so make sure they get lots to drink. Rainforest plants live in very humid conditions where they can get water directly from the air, even during drier spells, so keep the humidity up with a good mist. These guys love good drainage so don't let them get waterlogged, and repot in spring.

How not to kill your philodendron
While it is normal for older leaves to turn yellow, watch out for changes in colour as this may be a sign of distress! If lots of leaves go yellow, your plant could be getting too much light or is being over watered. Under watering will turn the leaves brown and they will fall off! Just stick to a good drink once a week and always let it dry out in between. No new growth means this tree lover is cold! Move it somewhere warmer.

THE BIG CHEESE

Cheese plant
Monstera deliciosa

Rating
Nothing cheesy about this easy pleaser.

Name check
The cheese plant gets its nickname from the big holes in its leaves. Easy peasy. As for the Latin name, think of something big lurking in the jungle. No, not Tarzan, a monster – raa!

The deets
With strong roots in the 1970s, the cheese plant brings mixed waves of nostalgia. While I fondly think of my nonna's plant taking over the living room, my sister's boyfriend hates them because they remind him of his geography teacher. But no matter how mean we are to the cheese plant, it will forgive you. This is the perfect flatmate for a beginner, and it's definitely a grower. People come to my shop and worry about the space, but I love big plants: they make a statement and look wicked. If you run out of room, start training the leaves around a picture frame. It's all about the lovely, large, leathery leaves, which you should wipe regularly to keep them clean and your cheese plant happy (see page 198). I also love using single leaves as flower displays – simply cut them off at the stem and sit in water.

Back to the roots
Think Rambo – hot, sweaty (and hunky). This guy started life on the forest floor, using aerial roots to attach itself to the trunks and branches of other trees to climb up towards the light. Even in your sitting room, your plant will produce these roots – attach them to a moss stick to help your cheese plant baby grow into a heartthrob. Back in the rainforest, the canopy of trees stops any direct sunlight getting through to the cheese plant below. With this is mind, consider where your plant will be happy: it loves light but doesn't need too much and won't like direct sunlight. Turn your pot around regularly, too, so the light reaches all the plant to help it grow straight and tall. You'll know if your cheese plant isn't getting enough light as the leaves will grow smaller and without holes. When it comes to watering, it can survive a little oversight – just don't make it a habit. Touch the soil and water when the compost feels dry, and reduce watering in winter when it goes into its chill-out phase. Also consider how humid it is back home and mist the leaves once a week to raise humidity levels. If your cheese plant isn't getting enough humidity, the leaves may start crisping. Keep them away from radiators so the temperature stays consistent. To keep it looking good, cut off dead leaves just above the base of the leaf's stem. Repot every few years, in spring, before new leaves appear.

How not to kill your cheese plant
Confusingly, when cheese plants don't get enough light, young leaves can start to grow towards dark spots rather than the light. This is because back in the rainforest, the darkest spots are where the tall trees are. The little shoots reach for them to clamber up into the light. Clever things. In our homes, the dark spots stay dark, so wrap them back into the main stems and get the poor thing some light. Yellow lower leaves can mean it's too cold. If the yellow leaves have brown tips, it's almost certainly caused by very dry air. Cut the dead brown bits off and get the mister out.

HOW TO GROW A F'ING HUGE PLANT UP YOUR WALL

I love letting my indoor jungle go wild, filling up any space it can get its leaves on (plants aren't polite when it comes to room). But when I started growing vines, I wasn't prepared for my jungle to get that massive. Wicked. Vines can climb their way across shelves, windowsills, doorways and, with a helping hand, the whole f'ing wall!

There a lots of different types of vines you can grow, but by far the easiest is devil's ivy. A climber rather than a vine, devil's ivy comes from the hot and humid rainforest where it has adapted to grow aerial roots to cling onto trees and climb up to the light. In its native habitat the vines can grow up to 12m, but in your small one-bed apartment you should be able to get a good 2.5m.

Devil's ivy is seriously easy to grow. It prefers indirect light and will adapt well to low-light rooms. Water sparingly when you see the leaves wilting. These guys hate soggy bottoms, and if the leaves turn yellow or keep falling, you're making things too wet. Remember to take it back to its warm roots by giving it good misting now and again, too.

Devil's ivy also gets bonus points for purifying the air in your home – according to NASA (yes, NASA!), the leaves remove harmful substances from the air.

Grow Up!
To help your devil's ivy grow you will need to help its aerial roots to attach to something. I put nails into my wall, wound non-rusting wire around them and let the plant go free. If you want the shoots to have a better hold, you can fasten them loosely to the support with string. Don't be too precious with it though: twist and trail it around different objects and supports. Your vine will always surprise you, going where it likes, separating and finding itself again and sometimes stubbornly refusing to shift. Be patient and keep going; it will get the hang of it after a while. Climbers can get big and heavy, so make sure they won't pull at their support. If you are renting, you can fix a trellis to the wall and remove it when you leave. To help it grow, cut it back a couple of times a year.

DESERT

Desert plants
* Succulents
* Cacti
* Yucca
* Agave
* (Tequila, anyone?)

When we think of the desert, we need to clear up a few misconceptions (I'm looking at you, Road Runner).

No. 1: desert plants don't grow in sand. They grow in a mixture of sand and soil, which drains very quickly meaning they never have soggy bottoms.

No. 2: it rains – but not very often. Most desert-dwellers have evolved over thousands of years to adapt to these unpredictable weather forecasts, cleverly storing water in their tissue when they can get it – this is why succulent leaves look like they're almost ready to burst! Many plants from the desert have also developed a waxy skin to seal in moisture and, instead of growing leaves, cacti have grown prickly spines (which have a smaller surface area than regular leaves) so they lose less precious water when they sweat. You might think cacti would grow deep roots to search for water underground, but instead they spread out shallow roots ready to absorb as much water as possible from the surface. When it does rain, they shoot out more roots but during dry spouts, their roots shrivel up and break off to conserve their water supply. Strong desert winds also mean the air is very dry so desert plants are used to really fresh, non-humid air.

No. 3: and we can all agree on this one – the desert is blazing hot! But did you know, it also gets really cold? During the day, all that intense sunlight heats the ground but at night that heat escapes, and the temperature in the desert drops very low. Cacti have adapted to survive in the sun's full glare by growing spines and hair which help shade the plant itself, and the cooler temperature at night helps them to retain water. Not just a prickly face!

So what have we learnt?
Desert dwellers have learnt to survive on very little water, so put that watering can down. They also need very good draining soil to prevent soggy bottoms. They LOVE sunshine in the day but they also like much cooler temperatures at night. Give them as much fresh air as possible and avoid humid environments like steamy bathrooms.

Desert gaffs
- Bright windowsills where sun lovers can sunbathe
- Sunny south-facing windowsills – but watch out for scorching
- Parts of the gaff that get cold at night
- Open terrariums make perfect desertscapes (see page 63)

MONDAYS SUCC!

Succulents
Sucus

Rating
Won't let you down, so don't let them drown.

Name check
Succulents literally 'suck' up water and store it. Look for fat juicy leaves and stems that look like they could burst if you squished them.

My top five succulents
- Burro's tail (*Sedum morganianum*)
- Jade plant (*Crassula ovata*)
- Agave (*Agave*)
- Houseleek (*Sempervivum*)
- String of pearls (*Senecio rowleyanus*)

The deets
Yes, they look cute when they are small, but believe me, these guys can grow up to be ugly. Personally, I love it, but I always say to my clients, a succulent is for life not for Christmas. Still interested? Read on.

Back to the roots
Succulents have evolved in dry areas of the world so they love free-draining soil, sunshine and fresh air. Sounds familiar? No, not really! Our wet and windy climate is just too damp for these guys. But they are surprisingly low maintenance. For the best chance of survival, keep on a sunny windowsill – there is no compromise – just be careful it's not getting scorched by direct sunlight through the glass. They can withstand long periods of drought by storing moisture in their leaves, stems and roots (which also helps them resist the desert heat), so don't worry if you forget to water them. Just don't make it a habit.

How not to kill your succulents
There will always be a leaf that is struggling – just snip it off and let the others flourish. But if the leaves fall off with a slight bump, watch the watering! Remember, they store water in their leaves, so if they are drinking too much, they will get too heavy and fall off. Over watering will also create soft black spots on the leaves or stem. If you start to notice the upper leaves are wrinkling (like they've been in the bath too long) or get dry and crispy, these guys need a good drink.

Styling with succulents
Succulents look best in groups like one big happy desert family, either in separate pots or in a large round bowl. Play with different shapes and textures, mixing spiky with fleshy!

Echeveria
This is nature showing off her graphic design skills: bold shapes, mad angles and a range of colours to match. This sassy succulent produces babies in abundance. If things get too crowded, propagate (see page 215).

Aeoniums
These have wicked shapes and woody stems that give them height. Look out for the black variety. So. Chic. Unlike other succulents, their extra-shallow root systems mean they cannot be allowed to dry out completely.

Jade plants
These have thicker stems and grow a bit like trees. If you're lucky they will produce tiny pink or white flowers. They are also known as money trees, so those of a superstitious nature should look after them carefully.

Cacti. Succulents. Wait, what's the difference?
Succulents are plants that store water in their leaves. The succulent family
is massive, but cacti are definitely the favourite child. These guys are distinguished
by a small cushion-like growth that usually develops spikes.
Some cacti won't have spikes but they will still have the cushiony growth
from where their great-great-great-grandpa cacti would have had them.

DON'T LET THE PRICKS INTIMIDATE YOU!

Cacti
Cactaceae

Rating
You say cact–i? We say cact–can!

Name check
There are so many species of cacti, it would be impossible to name them all. Learn your faves, they'll come to be the ones you know, love and call by name.

My top five cacti
- Golden barrel cactus (*Echinocactus grusonii*)
- Old man cactus (*Cephalocereus senilis*)
- Blue myrtle cactus (*Myrtillocactus geometrizans*)
- Mickey Mouse ears cactus (*Opuntia microdasys*)
- Peruvian apple cactus (*Cereus Peruvianus*)

The deets
I like to think of myself as a bit of a cactus collector, hunting for different textures, colours, shapes and sizes – and the wonkier the better. Despite their spiky exteriors, cacti are seriously laid back. The majority of cacti grow in the desert (desert cacti) where there is bright sunshine, high temperatures and dry air, although there are some species that grow in rainforests (forest cacti) that need shade and humidity.

As a general rule of pricked thumb, forest cacti can be recognised by their flat, trailing leaves, so when it comes to looking after your cacti, make sure you do your research first. We're concentrating on the desert variety here, so sunscreen on, we're going in.

Back to the roots
In the desert, cacti sometimes have to wait years for their next drink, so whatever you do, don't over water and never re-water until the compost is completely dry. My advice is to get to know your cactus: when cacti are watered their bodies swell and become firmer to the touch. See how heavy your cactus is and if it feels lighter than usual, top it up. They like well-draining soil to keep their roots nice and dry, so potting soil just ain't gonna cut it. Opt for cacti soil instead. Give them as much sunshine as possible, but watch direct sun in summer because your window can magnify the sun's rays and cook your cacti! They are happy with average heat in the day and cool nights. Deserts tend to be dry with low levels of humidity, so lose the mister. When it comes to feed, it depends on the type of cacti – most enjoy a meal once a month in summer.

How to repot your prickly cacti
In the wild, cacti have developed spikes to ward off predators and they might not realise you're one of the good guys! Wrap folded newspaper around the plant to move it between pots. Bubble wrap also works a treat. Repot small pots every year and bigger ones every two to three years. Never use too large a pot – the excess compost will make it damp and unhappy, so 3–5cm wider is fine.

How not to kill your cacti
If your cactus starts looking soft it is probably suffering from root rot. Check the roots and remove any slushy, mouldy-looking parts and hold back on the drink (see also page 209). If your cactus goes rubbery and discoloured, it's thirsty. Give it a good water but let the soil dry out before you give it another drink.

YOU SAY TERRANIUM,
I SAY WTF IS THAT? IT'S
NOT EVEN A WORD!

The terrarium is sexy and it knows it. Vessels of every shape and size create mini microclimates so your plants can get back to their roots! Let's get one thing straight before we start though: they are not called 'terraniums', repeat *not* 'terraniums' – at least 8/10 people call them that! At Grace & Thorn we hold Terrarium Tuesdays, but now you can make one on any day of the week! Follow our step-by-step guide to create your own miniature jungle for humid-loving plants or desert landscape for sunny succulents. Dinosaurs not included.

A potted history
In the 1800s, a hobbiest botanist, Dr Ward needed a case for his moth and caterpillar collection. While experimenting with a covered jar, he noticed a fern was growing in the soil in the jar's base. The Ward Case revolutionised planting, as it allowed plants from all over the world to be transported without damage. This sprouted the Victorians' plant obsession and soon no self-respecting household was without a terrarium. From miniature Taj Mahals to Brighton Pavilions, the Victorians went big and bold. Bravo! After World War II, leftover containers made from glass created a renewed spark in growing. Today, terrariums allow anyone with a little space, light and water to grow jungles and deserts in the middle of the city. They are great for modern housing, unfazed by air-conditioned or centrally heated homes.

Back to the roots
The reason plants are so happy in terrariums is because they create a microclimate that almost perfectly mimics the plant's roots – where it comes from. There are two main types of terrarium: open and closed. The open ones create a bright, dry desert-like landscape, great for sun-loving plants like succulents. A closed one can get nicely warm and humid, like a tropical rainforest. Humidity-loving plants will thrive here, so think ferns and moss that come from the forest floor. It is important not to mix plants with different roots together, as you will not be able to give them their individual needs.

Terrariums are the perfect way to learn about plants through trial and error – some may thrive while others may perish. Also, remember that like all plants, they will grow! When plants get too big, repot them and introduce them to your plant family.

The terrarium test
– Never over water – neglect is better than over caring!
– Place in a bright area, but not in direct sunlight. If you can read a book there, you're good
– When plant gets too big, either cut them back or repot into a bigger container
– Do not fertilise
– Refresh soil by scraping off the top layer and adding a fresh batch

HOW TO MAKE A CLOSED TERRARIUM – THE RAINFORST

Here comes the science bit. Concentrate! Water evaporating from the plant's leaves condenses onto the glass of your closed terrarium. This then trickles down the sides and is reabsorbed by the roots. This creates an ecosystem, allowing the plants to look after themselves.

Step 1. Choosing a vessel
Decide on your humidity hangout. This can be anything glass that has a lid or small opening – but note that these are a little harder to get plants in!

Step 2. Choosing plants
Humidity-lovin' plants. Ferns are going to thrive in these conditions. Moss also loves damp conditions and looks wicked. Before you get planting, group your chosen plants together and make sure you are happy with the heights, colours and textures.

Step 3. Drainage
Place some gravel or stones at the bottom of your chosen vessel. Although they are not as fussy as cacti, these plants like good drainage, too. It's also important to prevent the roots of your plants from getting damp and rotting.

Step 4. Soil
Add a layer of soil. A good potting compost will do. This doesn't have to be perfectly flat – you can create hills and mounds to give your mini landscape character.

Step 5. Making roots
Put your plants in their place! Using the back of a spoon make holes in the soil to plant your succulents. Make sure they are well rooted by firmly patting the soil around the plant.

Step 6. Setting the scene
Let your imagination run free. You can add lots of different things to decorate the top layer of your terrarium. We love using gravel, moss, twigs, pebbles and driftwood to create natural landscapes and models of people, animals, and even a prehistoric pal to add a little twist.

Step 7. Look after it
You both deserve a drink. Maintaining a closed terrarium is easy because it creates its own ecosystem. Place away from direct light and make sure it doesn't dry out by misting and watering once a month. Once you have a good system going, it requires little care and can thrive on neglect!

HOW TO MAKE AN OPEN TERRARIUM – THE DESERT

If you want to keep the terrarium vibe but for your mini desert plants that hate humidity, use an open vessel. There is no chance of things getting hot and sweaty but it will still create a nice little sun trap for them to feel right at home. Just watch out you don't cook your plants as the glass can get really hot.

Step 1: Choosing a vessel
First decide on your terrarium home. This can be anything from a mason or pickle jar to a vintage vase or even a fishbowl! Be daring. Because we are recreating desert roots, make sure fresh air can get in. So no lid.

Step 2: Choosing plants
Buy small, slow-growing plants. I use succulents and cacti for my desert ones. Don't over plant though – your plant babies need room to grow. Play around with different textures and heights before you get ready to plant them in! Grouping is key!

Step 3: Drainage
Place some gravel or stones at the bottom of your chosen vessel. Cacti hate soggy bottoms! This layer aids drainage and helps to prevent the roots of your plants from getting damp and rotting.

Step 4: Soil
Add a layer of soil (cactus soil for your desert). It doesn't have to be a perfectly flat layer – create hills and mounds to give your mini landscape some character.

Step 5: Making roots
Put your plants in their place! Using the back of a spoon make holes in the soil to plant your succulents. Make sure they are well rooted by firmly patting the soil around the plant.

Step 6: Setting the scene
Let your imagination run free! You can add lots of different things to decorate the top layer of your terrarium. We love using gravel, moss, twigs, pebbles and driftwood to create natural landscapes and models of people, animals and even a few dinosaurs to add a little twist.

Step 7: Look after it
You both deserve a drink. Maintaining a terrarium is easy – the trick is to not to over water. For an open terrarium we recommend a good spritz once a month. Make sure it gets lots of light, too, but watch out for direct sun that can scorch the leaves through the glass.

SUBTROPICS

Subtropical plants
* Kentia palm
* Spider plant
* Beefsteak
* Asparagus fern
* Oxalis

Most of the houseplants we know and love come from subtropical climes. So how are we defining this group of plants? Basically, it is the chill out mix.

Hailing from the Americas to China and Australia to South East Asia, these are the plants with super holiday vibes. Unlike our hard-grafting rainforest friends who have had to adapt to the damp and dark undergrowth and fight for light through the canopy of the trees, these subtropical guys are just chilling. Coming from close to the equator, these plants get sun pretty much all year round and can adapt to different levels of intensity. Palms, like the kentia, have developed their wide fronds to catch the sun's rays without scorching, while many smaller plants will hang out in their partial shade below, so will love light – but they won't like being scorched. When you plan your faraway hols, think about how the rainy seasons might put a dampener on when you go. These plants are used to lots of rain but they have also adapted to dry spells, too. And humidity? It wouldn't be a holiday without it, but as there is no canopy of trees above them to trap in the humidity, they are easy-going about it, too. And, unlike in the rainforest, subtropical climates have seasons! Well, two to be exact: a hot, humid summer and a mild, cool winter. So, that means they are tolerant to a wide range of temperatures, enjoying a bit of a chill in the winter months.

So what have we learnt?
Instead of climbing up to catch the light like their rainforest pals, these guys have enough light to go round so can adapt to both bright and indirect spots, but watch out for scorching. Humidity is high, but it doesn't get trapped by the trees above, so they aren't going to love your bathroom as much as rainforest plants. Subtropical dwellers get regular rain but have also adapted to dry spells so you can be more relaxed with the watering. And because they have seasons, turn up the chill over Christmas.

Subtropical gaffs
- Chill out zones with sun and shade
- Humid bathrooms (but let your rainforest plants go to the front of the queue)
- An east-facing window will stop plants getting scorched

INCY WINCY SPIDER PLANT

Spider plant
Chlorophytum comosum

Rating
Not an incy wincy bit difficult.

Name check
A spider with lots of hanging legs.

The deets
One of my absolute faves, it upsets me how unpopular they are. Let's give the spider plant some love! It is one of the easiest houseplants to grow because it will put up with changes in light, feed and temperature without much fuss. It is also relatively free of disease and pests. Plus, you buy one plant and you end up with ten! Fancy a spider plant waterfall? Plant several babies in a big enough hanger and watch them giggle as they cascade down!

Back to the roots
Hailing from tropical and southern regions of Africa, it loves light. I had one in a basement flat and it struggled. When it's happy, it grows quickly and has lots of babies. They love a drink, but give them a detox in the winter. Feed once a month. They also enjoy a mist.

How to grow baby spider plants
When you start to see roots, snip the baby off right next to the stem, pot into moist compost, give it a good drink and put in a bright spot away from direct light. Keep it moist and in a few weeks, you will see the leaves grow! Aww. If your spider plant isn't producing babies, your plant is probably too young – you'll just have to wait. Another reason could be that its pot is too small so try repotting.

How not to kill your spider plant
Spider plants are particularly hard to kill, but there are a few tell-tale signs that it's not happy. If the ends of the leaves go brown, it's probably too hot. Make sure it's not above a radiator or give it somewhere with better fresh air. It could also need a feed. Once the ends have gone brown they won't go green again so nip them off. If the leaves start losing their streak in winter, you are over watering.

Nik's spider plant story
Every so often, an extraordinary lady comes into the shop, dressed in the oldest tracksuit you've ever seen and slippers. She shuffles through the foliage as slow as a snail. The first time, I watched, a little baffled, as she picked up plant after plant after plant, and took them up to the till. The lot came to 300 quid, and before I knew it she'd disappeared down the road in a black cab! Now, whenever she's in, I whisper to my girls, 'Just you watch'. She always buys a spider plant. I imagine her at home, in a millionaire's pad, with an overflowing spider plant waterfall.

PALM SUNDAY

Palms
Arecaceae

Rating
Seriously L.A.id back.

Name check
The term 'palm' is given to plants that have a cluster of leaves at the top of a stem or trunk. In other words, a pole with hair.

My top five palms
- Kentia palm (*Howea forsteriana*)
- Parlour palm (*Chamaedorea elegans*)
- Jade Empress palm (*Rhapis multifida*)
- European fan palm (*Chamaerops humilis*)
- Face palm (ouch)

The deets
Palms are the DeLorean time-machine of the plant world, transporting us back to colonial eras and glamorous hotels. I love draping their leaves, spreading them out over the room in great big layers. Size always matters! Stick a big statement plant in a small space

– it will pack a punch and immediately make the room feel bigger! At Grace & Thorn we love a kentia palm – they look so classic, but they are not the most forgiving. If you mistreat them, you'll see straightaway. I am forever chopping off brown leaves but more often than not the leaves come back.

Back to the roots
While palm trees may evoke visions of Californian girls, not a single one is native to the City of Angels. Palms can be found in nearly all warm parts of the world because they love heat, but they are most common in the wettest parts of the subtropics. Large, fan-shaped leaves are designed to catch sunshine and water and the leaves are segmented, so excess water can drain away. Palms love light, so try to give them a sunny spot, but watch out for sunburn as their leaves can easily scorch. They are adaptable though, so they will be OK in darker spaces, too. You'll soon know if it's not getting enough light, as the leaves will stretch out to reach for the sun. Palms' 'trunks' are covered in cork-like layers, which protect their insides from the heat. Because of their wet pasts, they require continual watering, so thoroughly soak them – they love a bath in the summer, but don't let them get soggy. They also love humidity, so mist regularly but hold back in the winter.

How not to kill your palm
The palm's leaves should be healthy and dark green. If they go brown, it could mean the air is too dry so keep up the misting. If they are thirsty, their leaves will turn yellow. Because of their big leaves, palms easily collect dust. This can slow down photosynthesis so misting will also help keep them clean.

Rating
Happy raver.

Name check
Three is the magic number when it comes *Oxalis triangularis*, which has three common names: false shamrock, purple shamrock and love plant.

The deets
This bulb plant loves to dance. You know I love nature that dances and this beauty raves like no one's business. It has three purple heart-shaped leaves that sit symmetrically to one another at the end of every stem. When the plant blooms, it produces lots of little white flowers. Their leaves are light sensitive, so after they have finished dancing in the sun all day, their leaves will close at night when the sun goes down.

Back to the roots
Oxalis triangularis is native to South Africa and South America – it is endemic in Brazil, meaning it grows EVERYWHERE! It grows naturally among rocks near streams, but easily naturalises in disturbed sites, on the edge of woodlands and near gardens in subtropical and warm temperate areas. So it feels at home, keep this one in the sun on the sunniest windowsill you have (stick him outside in the summer, too, but not if above 24°C). Because this is a bulb plant, don't allow the plant to get soggy. Allow the top 2.5cm of soil to dry out between watering (think rocks keeping it dry over the stream).

Blooming lovely
A healthy oxalis will reward you with lots of beautiful leaves and white flowers. Feed every two weeks while the plant is growing with a liquid fertiliser diluted by half. When blooming stops, feed every other month.

How not to kill your Oxalis
This plant can revive itself from the dead! Like other plants grown from bulbs, the purple shamrock requires one or more 'rest period' each year, particularly during the autumn. If your plant looks tired after it blossoms, stop watering it and let it go dormant for about a month. When it perks up and comes back to life, feed and water as usual.

You will not typically see many pests on oxalis. Check under the leaves for aphids, spider mites and other pests before bringing it into your home and you should be fine. If you ever do end up with an infestation you can't get a handle on, simply wait until the plant goes dormant again. Remove all the leaf litter and the bugs are gone!

CLUB MED

Club Med plants
* Scented geraniums
* Jasmine
* Lemon tree

So... ahem, I've developed a bit of an obsession with taking photos of plants abroad. My mates are forever taking the mick out of me on hols as they will often lose me on a walk and then find me up a side road taking photos of plants! I just love seeing the plants we have as houseplants out and about!

Mediterranean plants are all about colour and scent. They are a chance to turn your concrete walls into a mini oasis. When it comes to selecting pots, think brightly painted terracotta urns, patterned tiles and old vintage vessels. If space permits, add a small table and a chair or two to create your very own sanctuary, away from the hustle and bustle of everyday life.

The Mediterranean climate consists of hot, dry summers and mild, wet winters. This means many Mediterranean natives are tolerant of dry air and dry-ish soil, making them adaptable houseplants. Keep plants that hail from the heat in the sunniest place in your house and if you decide to put them outside in the summer, remember they've probably never seen snow, so move back in before the frost comes. Water well in the summer but make sure they have good drainage as they will hate being wet. Watch the drink in the winter – these guys might still be thirsty.

So what have we learnt?
Give these plants a sunny spot on your windowsill to remind them of their Mediterranean sunbathing roots. If you put them outside, don't forget to bring them inside again at the first hint of frost – they don't like the cold! Don't forget to give them a good drink, and keep an eye on them in winter, too, but let them dry out before watering again.

Club Med gaffs
- Sunny windowsills for light lovers
- Outside spaces for fresh air lovers and balconies where buds can bloom – but bring them inside in winter as they don't like to chill.

SMELLS LIKE SCENTED GERANIUMS

Scented geraniums
Pelargonium

Rating
Happy when in full sun with regular drinks (who isn't?).

Name check
Learn how to identify geraniums and then rub their leaves: if it's fragrant, it's scented.

The deets
I remember the smell of scented geraniums at my nonna's when I was a child. She had them at the front, back and inside the house. Everywhere! But don't be fooled into thinking these are fuddy-duddy plants – if you have never experienced a scented geranium

you're in for a treat. What's amazing about these plants is that they mimic other scents – rose, lemon, lime, pine, chocolate and even coconut. SO on trend! Although they do sometimes bloom, scented geraniums are grown for their fragrant leaves. I love the textures and shapes of the leaves, too; there is so much variety. To release the scent, you crush the leaves or simply give them a ruffle when passing by. They were particularly favoured by the Victorians when the fragrant leaves were added to finger bowls for guests to rinse their hands in between courses at dinner. Oh, and you can eat them, too!

Back to the roots
They like lots of sun. Sunny balconies and outdoor spaces are perfect, but they will do just as well on a sunny windowsill indoors. They aren't very fussy about soil type, although they don't like soggy bottoms so make sure they can drain well. Neglect is much better than over watering – just give them a regular good drink and let them dry out before watering again. Think of those warm(ish) Mediterranean winters, so don't let things get frosty. These guys love a good haircut too; don't be shy, you won't do it any damage by giving it a good trim now and then, just watch out for any growing tips.

How not to kill your scented geranium
In general, these guys are pretty easy to look after and mostly pest free. Regular watering, a little food and haircuts will keep your plant babies healthy and strong. Discoloured leaves may be a sign that the plant is 'hungry' and is short of food, or check that the plant is not too wet. Drain the pot well and allow the plant to dry out a bit before re-watering.

AND ALL THAT JASMINE

Jasmine
Jasminum

Rating
Smooth (sun worshipper) when watered
regularly.

Name check
The word jasmine comes from the Arabic
word *yasmin*, meaning gift from God. Once
you smell a jasmine, you're not likely to forget
it. Go for a sniff to identify.

The deets
One thing I love most about the Med is the
night air. It is almost alive with scents that drift
past as you sit outside, G & T in one hand
and good gardening book in the other. I am
always intoxicated by the scent of jasmine –
soft, sweet and sultry. Go for the *Jasminum
polyanthum*, which is perfect for growing
indoors. It flowers in winter and is particularly
fragrant at night. Bliss.

Back to the roots
There are over two hundred species of
jasmine, which hail from the olive family.
A holiday lover at heart, the jasmine prefers
bright light with some direct sun in the summer
– bagsy its perfect sun-bathing spot on a
south-facing windowsill. The most important
thing to remember when growing jasmine
indoors is temperature: in the summer they
will be happy in the sun, BUT when they go
into flowering over the winter they hate being
hot, so make sure they are not near radiators
and avoid humid bathrooms. When it comes
to watering, these guys like a drink so try to
keep the soil moist but not soggy. They get
really thirsty when they are flowering and
if you let them dry out, so will the blooms.
If your jasmine isn't flowering, check your
conditions. Jasmines are climbers so will need
support to grow – I love trailing mine around
the window to get my fragrant fix.

How not to kill your jasmine
If you don't give it enough water, the leaves
and flowers will turn brown. Pruning your
jasmine is important to keep it healthy. Prune
back after flowering and don't leave it too
late, as you'll chop off the next crop!

Let life give you lemons
If I close my eyes, I'm in Sicily – glass of wine in one hand, watering can in the other. When I open them, OK, I might be in drizzly London but the lemon tree in front of me is a happy reminder of sunnier climates and lots of good plonk. Many lemons that grow in the Mediterranean won't mind life as a houseplant, as long as you give them plenty of sun and a large pot with good drainage.

6 Move to a sunny spot and follow the care guide on page 250.

5 When you spy shoots, you're lemon tree is ready to grow!

4 Leave in a warm, dark place and wait for shoots to appear.

GROW YOUR OWN LEMON TREE

Water well and keep the soil moist with a daily mist. Keep them outdoors in the summer to make them feel at home and then bring them in for the winter. If you want to go straight to tree territory, go for dwarf varieties like the hardy Meyer lemon, which produces pretty blossom in spring and is said to be bountiful. Look for plants that are at least two to three years old, as these give you fruit right away. *Buon appetito!*

Or, why not try growing your own citrus tree from a pip? It's a great project and a lot cheaper than plane tickets:

3 In the morning, pot up a small container and press each pip 1.5cm into the compost.

2 Pour the rest of the Shiraz for you and pour some water for the pips. Soak overnight.

1 Take a healthy lemon, squeeze over your fusilli supper and keep the pips.

THE BOG

Bog plants
* Venus flytrap
* Giant pitcher plant
* Yellow pitcher plant
* Butterwort
* Cobra lily
* Ferns

No, I don't mean the downstairs loo (although a client of mine actually thought that's what I meant when I told her that pitcher plants were bog plants – oh, how I laughed!), I mean the wet swampy kind of climate a few of my favourite houseplants come from. And, while I don't expect you to have a swamp in your home, to house some of the weirdest and most wonderful plants on the planet you're gonna have to think a bit weird and wonderfully.

Swamps and marshes are generally found in warmer climates, while bogs are more common to cold or even Arctic areas in North America, Europe and Asia. They also exist at high altitudes in warmer regions, such as the Sierra Nevada in America. The bog is a self-explanatory microclimate: fresh boggy undergrowth, damp, humid and very wet. One of the main features of a boggy area is that water is constantly running above or below ground level. Now, while this may sound like a houseplant's wet dream, this constant flow of water can wash away nutrients in the soil, hence why some plants that are native to swamps – like the carnivorous varieties coming up on the next page – have adapted to find nutrients elsewhere. Or insects to be more precise. Plants adapted to swampy bog life are almost constantly near water so keep their soil damp at all times and make sure they never dry out.

Ferns are also big in the bog world and one beauty is called the *Osmundastrum cinnamomeum* aka cinnamon fern. It is a epiphyte, which means it grows harmlessly on other plants, such as on a neighbouring tree, getting its moisture and nutrients from the air, rain and sometimes the debris that accumulates around it – clever! As we know, ferns love similar, moist conditions found on the rainforest floor, so also check out some suitable fern flatmates on page 48.

So what have we learnt?
Bog plants like it wet. I like to test my plants sometimes and left a pitcher plant for a few days and boy it didn't like it at all, it went all shrivelled. Keep them soggy people! A lack of nutrients in their boggy soil means they use more energy from the sun, so make sure they are getting enough light – but don't scorch them.

Bog gaffs
- Rooms with water for big drinkers
- Moist bathrooms for damp dwellers
- East-facing windows for the easily sunburnt

CARNIVOROUS PLANTS

Watch out: insect-eating plants are high maintenance, mainly in their desire for fancy water and lots of it. That's right, these guys don't just ask for tap water. They've evolved to receive nutrients from food, so you can't cheat with ordinary water, as it contains salts that will burn their sensitive roots. If you're not feeling flush, just use cooled down boiled water. Because their swamp habits wash away all the nutrients in their soil, carnivorous plants survive by eating insects instead. To attract their prey, they produce a scent or nectar, and then the ill-fated insect becomes trapped in the plant's structure or gets stuck to its sticky coat. Once the insect is ensnared, the plant uses enzymes to break the insect down into the nutrients it needs. Yum!

Most insect-eating plants are used to damp conditions but because of the constant flow of water, they like soil that drains well. As their natural soil lacks nutrients, these guys hate being overfed, so avoid potting mix – it will be too rich for them to digest. Insect-eating plants need lots of light to keep their digestive systems working well but keep away from direct sources. And I've gotta say it... don't feed plants with cat food, take-away leftovers or bits from your roast dinner! Toss in the occasional dead fly, if that's your kind of thing, but only if it is fresh.

Flytraps
Who? The Venus flytrap is the infamous bad boy of this category.
How? These guys have hinged leaves that open and close to trap insects. Chomp.
Watch out! Don't 'tease' it, by tickling the plant to make it snap shut, this weakens the plant, and if you do it too much, you can kill it.

Pitchers
Who? Pitcher plant.
How? They have water-filled funnels that the insects fall down and drown, slowly.
Watch out! There are many types of pitcher plants with many different needs. Some varieties can be a little fussy so always do your homework.

Sticky-leaved plants
Who? Butterworts (*Pinguicula*).
How? These silent killers attract and capture insects with a sticky sap on their stems.
Watch out! The word *pinguicula* translates as 'little greasy one', which refers to the substance resembling grease on their leaves.

How not to kill your carnivorous plants
When carnivorous plants chill out in the winter, it's natural for them to dry out a bit. Don't panic if the traps or leaves start dying, just snip them off at the base when they are yellow or brown. Watch out for greenfly, too – these pests escape those carnivorous jaws!

Fun fact!
The pitcher plant got its nickname by being a handy drinking
vessel for parched monkeys – and sometimes even thirsty
humans – looking for refreshment in the heat!

UP IN THE AIR PLANTS

Air plants
Tillandsias

Rating
Strangely easy.

Name check
Plants that grow in the air. Obvs.

The deets
Plants that can grow without soil? Far out! Air plants are weird and wonderful creatures with out-of-this-world qualities that have adapted over thousands of years to survive. And, despite their alien qualities, these guys are so damn cute! Often poufy, always graceful, they blush before they bloom and have their own pups! What makes these plants so easy is that they take their water and nutrients from the air and use their roots as anchors to hang out anywhere. There are lots of different varieties to choose from with wicked textures, colours and blooms. And they range from teeny to huge! You can get really creative with styling them, from terrariums to wall displays. Or be like Grace & Thorn and attach them to your favourite plastic dinosaur (see over the page). The sky's the limit!

Back to the roots
Native to the Americas, air plants love warm weather, but they can thrive despite neglect, as these guys have evolved in diverse environments – from the tops of mountains to wet swamps – meaning they are pretty unfussy when it comes to finding a home. Tillandsia (or air plants to you and me) are a type of epiphytes – plants that grow on other things without harming them – so these guys can grow on practically anything! In the wild, the host plants shade them from direct sun, so a space with bright, indirect light, like a hallway, will be perfect. They get their moisture and nutrients from the air, rain and debris around them so don't worry about feed, but mist your air plants regularly to keep humidity levels high, especially if your gaff is air-conditioned – mist daily in the summer and once or twice a week in the winter. To store this valuable moisture, air plants have adapted to do their breathing at night. This amazing skill means that you should avoid watering your air plants at night so as not to interrupt them.

How to water an air plant
Rather than soaking the carpet, give it a bath in a bowl of water every few weeks. Make sure the plant is completely submerged and leave for half an hour, or however long your plant baby likes. Air plants only take up as much water as they need, so you won't over water by doing this. When bathtime is done, give it a shake upside down to dry off before hanging again. Be careful not to leave it damp as it can rot easily.

Aww cute pups!
Think of your air plant as the mum plant. Her babies are called 'pups'. Aww. A single mum plant can have up to a dozen pups so be prepared for your family to grow! To do this, place the mum plant in a bowl of water for 2–3 hours to hydrate it. Remove from the

water and gently spread the leaves with your fingers to reveal the little pups. Separate the pups from the mum by gently pulling them out from the base – don't pull them from their tips, which are fragile. Put the pups into the bowl of water to soak, then hang them close together and mist the pups twice a day.

Blooming lovely
As long as you are looking after your air plant baby it may well bloom. If you are super keen, look for plants that are starting to grow pups when you buy them. Tillandsia flower at maturity and will only bloom once in their life. Your plant (the mum) will start producing baby plants (the pups) when she is nearing maturity. She will then die off, but each pup will grow into a mature plant and flower. Blooms can last from days to months, depending on the species.

Styling air plants
The best part of owning air plants is how you style them in your home. Get creative. All you need to fix them to a surface is glue, staples or mesh wire. Do not not use Superglue or copper wire though, as these will kill your plant and don't staple the leaves!

How not to kill your air plants
The easiest way to kill an air plant is to leave it with a soggy bottom after watering. Always make sure you shake it off properly after bathtime, and let it dry out in a bright but indirect light. If you're still unsure, use a paper towel to remove excess water. If you notice your air plant is softer in colour, has rolled or wrinkled leaves, or browning tips, it's probably thirsty. Give it a good bath overnight. Don't panic if the bottom leaves turn brown, it's natural. Just snip them off to keep your air plant baby looking it's best.

HOW TO MAKE A DINO AIR PLANT

Nothing says Grace & Thorn like an air plant on a plastic dinosaur! No roots, no soil, no fear of extinction, these fuss-free dino air plants are super easy to care for and make a great alternative plant gift. Concentrating? Then we shall begin.

1   Take one glue gun.

2   Take one air plant.

3   Take one dinosaur (we like to hunt for ours on Amazon).

4   Stick air plant onto dinosaur with glue gun (make sure the glue is hidden).

5   # RUN!

6   Just kidding. You're good.

HOUSE RULES

The secret of co-habitation? Observe, observe, observe. Plants don't just die overnight. If you give them a little once over every Sunday morning, Bloody Mary in one hand and mister in the other (as I do), you will soon notice how they are doing. For happy plants, follow these rules.

1. DON'T PUT STYLE BEFORE SUCCULENT!

Or any other type of plant for that matter! Sure, that cactus will look fantastic in your basement, but if this sun-loving desert plant is getting no light, it will be miserable. Go back to its roots (see page 59) and put it where it will be happy. Don't panic, there will be alternative plants that love those conditions. Once you know what you can provide your plants, no space is too small! You can put them everywhere. Be daring. Don't be afraid to move plants around, but keep an eye on them. If they look unhappy in their new home, try somewhere else. Buddy up plants with similar needs to make it easier to look after them. Keep the relevant tools at hand in each room, from rainforest humidity-making misters in the sitting room to DIY fertilisers in the kitchen.

Psst! Take a leaf out of other people's plants
OK, not literally (although you can sometimes, see page 215). Looking at where other people keep plants happy is a shortcut to success. Is there a restaurant or estate agent's on your street with a big happy jade in the window? When you peer into your neighbour's front room (we all do it), do you spy a healthy fiddle fig? Does the balcony three floors down bloom with bamboo? Or is the girl with the desk opposite you smugly watering her cacti collection? If these people can grow those plants in those places – so can you.

2. LET THERE BE LIGHT.

So many people come into my shop asking if a plant can survive without light. The simple answer is, NO! CAN YOU? House rule no. 2: all plants need light to grow. Why? Time for the science bit, concentrate: plants combine carbon dioxide from the air with water from their soil to make the nutrients they need to survive. This is called photosynthesis. Still with me? For this process to happen properly, plants need energy, which they get from the sun. Without light, they won't get enough energy and will die. How much light a plant needs depends on how they have adapted in their native habitats – desert plants need full beams but some bog dwellers can survive on hardly any at all. But when I say 'hardly any at all' I don't mean none. Capiche?

Never eat shredded wheat

So now you know you need light, how much do you have in your home? First, you need to work out which way your windows face to understand how much light they get. Not sure how to do that? Just use the compass on your phone! Remember, even if you're south facing, have you got a massive tower block opposite? Make sure enough light is getting through that concrete view.

North-facing

Light: North-facing windows don't get much sun at all – think of them as a shady spot.
Watch out! Avoid putting sun lovers here, they won't be happy.
Hang out: Plants who don't like direct light will be very happy here.
Faves: Try a shade-loving Boston fern.

South-facing

Light: South-facing windows get the best of the sunshine.
Watch out! In the summer things can really hot up, so watch your plants don't scorch.
Hang out: This is the perfect place for sun-loving plants.
Faves: Sunbathing succulents.

East-facing

Light: East-facing windows get good amounts of light, but not as much as a westerly one.
Watch out! All that early morning light means it's more susceptible to frost.
Hang out: Plants that like indirect light will be A-OK.
Faves: Try an adaptable asparagus fern here.

West-facing

Light: West-facing windows get good, warm light, but less than their south-facing cousins.
Watch out! If it gets really sunny, west-facing light can also scorch.
Hang out: Plants that need bright, indirect light will thrive here.
Faves: The big cheese plant.

Don't forget to turn the lights off!

It is important to remember that most of the plants on this planet have evolved in a day-night cycle. Therefore, they need a period of darkness to develop properly. If that has now got you worrying about plants in offices where the lights are always left on, remember many tropical houseplants originate from along the equator where they get about 12 hours of glorious sun all day, every day. So 24 hours of weak office light will just about compensate. Still, poor things.

3. LET IT FLOW, LET IT FLOW!

Just like humans, plants need air to breathe, so make sure your plant has good ventilation. Keep your windows open in summer to let the fresh air in. Most houseplants hate draughts (don't we all?) so avoid keeping them somewhere they are constantly going to get blasted! If you live somewhere where you can't open the windows, air-conditioning should still create a good breeze, but don't put your plants near the vents.

4. HUMIDITY IS RISING...

When we talk about humidity, we are talking about the amount of vapour in the air. If we go back to the roots of our tropical houseplants, they have grown to adapt to humid environments and will need these conditions to thrive. Kitchens and bathrooms are great spots for humid-loving plants because of the constant blasts of steam, but if you want to keep your tropical plants in, say, the sitting room, you need to consider that when you turn the radiator on it evaporates the vapour in the air, meaning that a centrally heated room in winter can be as dry as the desert – see the problem? But before you grab the frizz-ease, there are easy ways to increase humidity just around your houseplants, from a pebble tray to the good old mister. Check into the Houseplant Hospital to find out more (see page 210).

5. IT'S GETTING HOT IN HERE.

Those tropical climates are nice and warm, so houseplants are much happier inside than if they were out in our gardens. Compared with the tropics though, the lower light and humidity levels means that our homes are actually a bit cooler, especially at night, but that doesn't mean you need to start going to bed with the heating on. Most of the unfussy guys in this book will be 'just right' at home. But there are a few things to consider:
- If you have old sash windows, watch that your plants don't get too cold in winter, or consider desert plants that are used to chilly nights.
- Changing seasons also affect the temperature in your home. Like people, plants need more to drink in thirsty weather – and watch out for strong summer sun as it can give plants sunstroke.
- Plants from tropical and Mediterranean climates are not used to frost, so make sure their leaves don't touch the windowpanes on cold winter nights.
- Avoid putting your plants near radiators, as the constant changes in temperature will upset them.

6. NO SPACE IS TOO SMALL.

Once you've found your plant sweet spot, fill it! You can get a lot of plants in that space, trust me. I should know: in my one-bed shoebox flat I had over 40 plants of all shapes and sizes. My steamy bathroom was full of humid-loving rainforest plants and I crammed cacti into all my sunny spaces. Not only does it look wicked, but it's useful, too – putting plants together increases humidity (see page 210) and you can keep an eye on the drink by watering them together. If you're looking at your tiny flat and thinking, no chance, remember, it's all about being creative with your space. The walls and ceiling have plant potential too! See Does My Cheese Plant Look Big in This (page 181) to get inspired.

ROOM GUIDE

A lot of people come into the shop looking for a plant for a specific room in their home and get despondent if it doesn't fair well there. Just move it elsewhere and try again! Draughts, sun, radiators etc. all play a part in your plants' happiness. Don't be afraid to move them until you find their happy spot.

RAINFOREST ROOMS

Bathroom botanics
Bathrooms are great for creating a hot, damp rainforest climate and humid-loving plants who hail from these conditions are going to be very happy here. Rainforest plants often live in low-lying areas, shaded by the trees, so you won't need much bright light either. If your window is frosted, but still gets some light, think of it like the dappled effect of a tree canopy. Experiment with hanging moisture-loving fittonias off shelves, or placing ferns around the bath. Forget succulents though: these are desert plants who watch what they drink and will be miserable here.

The unused fireplace
Perfect for creating low light conditions for the adaptable spider plant. Ferns will also love it in this dark corner, but remember to keep the humidity levels up with regular misting.

Wicked witch of the north-facing windowsill
North-facing windows don't get direct sunlight so are great for shade lovers from the rainforest floor. Look for plants that can adapt to low light conditions and particularly hate direct sun. The maidenhair fern, with her sensitive fronds, could relax here without worrying about getting scorched.

Fancy a cuppa?
Is there a lovely steamy shelf above your kettle? Try a humidity-loving plant up there. Don't put it too close, but close enough to get a lovely blast every time you fancy a brew. Invite the fit fittonia over for tea and see how steamy things can get!

Dig the dishes
Think of all that energy a dishwasher uses, creating a nice warm patch in the kitchen – not to mention all that lovely hot air that floats around every time you open the door. Try letting a humidity-loving bloodleaf plant hang out near your dirty pots and pans. This tropical dream is a little high maintenance but having it near water will suit it. Sadly, it doesn't do the dishes.

Swinging sitting room
I'm talking about sitting rooms with a window or two, so let's think about climates with bright but controlled light. Instead of those plants on the shaded rainforest floor, let's look at the ones climbing up towards the sun. These guys grow roots upwards to climb the trees, and the space in your sitting room will allow them to swing! Always shaded by the tree canopy, place them out of direct sun to ensure they are happy. As this is your main room, think big and statement: the big cheese of plants, the cheese plant, with its aerial roots, will thrive.

See the sky light
Plants native to the rainforest undergrowth, who have adapted to grow under the canopy may be very happy under a filtered or frosted skylight. A philodendron will be very content but remember that these guys like to climb, up, up, up towards the light, so be prepared to see it grow. Sun-lovin' succulents may also be happy hanging out in macramé under a sunny skylight (as long as it's not in the bathroom – too steamy). Try Burro's tail for the 'perfect from all angles' approach.

DESERT LANDSCAPES

South-facing windowsills
Succulents that hail from the hot, dry desert love a bright spot in your home with lots of fresh air. Your sunny windowsill is perfect. It is also handy to keep your cacti collection grouped together so you can keep an eye on them, making sure trips with the watering can are kept to a minimum. To make these guys really happy, let there be light! Rotate their pots so each side of the plant is getting rays. In summer, the window glass can refract and scorch your succulent sweethearts – if this looks like it's happening, move them where there is less direct sun but still plenty of light.

Sunny shelves
You know that spot on your wall that catches the sun? That, my friend, is a little succulent sweet spot. Time to get the drill out (seriously guys, you should know how to use one!) and set up a little shelf in its honour.

SUBTROPICAL SPACES

Holiday hang-outs
These plants are laid back and totally chilled out, taking life as it comes. Like us on holiday, they like a bit of sun, a bit of shade and a nice amount of humidity but they're basically easy going guys and they're pretty adaptable, too. If you have a sitting room or hallway that gets a nice amount of sun during the day but not too much direct light, then this is the spot for them. Plants that can tolerate lower light levels will do well, although palms like the kentia palm enjoy waving their leaves somewhere a bit brighter. Subtropical plants won't mind a humid bathroom either but settle your rainforest pals in there first.

CLUB MED DESTINATIONS

Get out!
Plants from the Med like sun, shade and good drainage. Geraniums and scented geraniums are personal faves. Not everyone is lucky enough to have an outside space for plants, but there may be more options available to you than you realise. What about the steps going up to your front door? A window ledge you could (carefully) fix a window box to? As long as it gets light and you can get to it regularly (and safely!) to water your plant babies, your garden will most certainly grow! Just remember to keep an eye on them and bring them indoors if it gets too cold.

THE BOG

Queue for the loo
Anywhere there is a water supply nearby is great for your bog plants. No excuse not to water them every day! Also, for the carnivorous, they appreciate an open window for their daily treat of flies!

UP, UP IN THE AIR

Hanging out in hallways
Hallways with good light but little space are the perfect home for air plants. These guys can hang out on the walls, leaving room for all the other things that seem to accumulate on the floor. And they won't get knocked by dogs barging in! Because many of them start their life living on trees, they're used to bright conditions with some shade. If the sun gets weak in winter, move them somewhere a little brighter. Just give them fresh air, water and make sure they don't get too cold.

MORE PLANT POSSIBILITIES

No lighty? No likey
OK, OK I get it – it's dark and dingy but you're desperate for a plant to help turn that room into your yoga studio. You have two options, plant friend. 1) You send your plant to plant perjury where it will die a slow and painful death and swap it out with a new one every three months. Cruel. 2) You swap your plants around with others in sunnier spots so it gets respite in the sun every once in a while. I don't advise this, as it's a pain and your plant is not gonna be happy.

Backed into a corner
No plant lover puts nothing in a corner! Don't let that empty space in your room go to waste. Some plants that originate from cool mountain forests actually enjoy being up against a wall – used to the shade from the trees, these guys require little light. Devil's ivy is a great option and that unused corner will soon become a plant-climbing paradise, as it spreads out to find the sun.

The downstairs loo
You will want to put plants that can thrive in darker conditions in this special place. A fern will be very happy here, but you'll have to keep a mister by its side to keep up humidity levels. A moss terrarium will also do the trick. If you've got the space, philodendrons can look pretty wicked, or what about an unfussy hanging spider plant?

King of the kitchen
Kitchens vary in light, temperature and humidity, but often they will have a bright sunny window. This is the perfect place to grow your own edible plants. From ridiculously easy-to-grow tomatoes or an avocado experiment to a chic indoor herb garden (see pages 124–125), not only is it practical for cooking, the amount of time generally spent in the kitchen means you can keep a closer eye on your DIY plant babies, making sure they'll grow big, strong and delicious. Growing plants need a lot of water, so having a tap to hand is extremely handy. Watch them every day when you're washing up and you'll soon get to know their drinking habits. *Buon appetito!*

Bedrooms with benefits
Life = Stressful. Plants = Peace. The bedroom, where we get our R&R, will benefit from a helping hand from plants that purify the air, helping you relax, sleep and be happy. Besides, there is nothing quite like waking up and being greeted by the waving leaves of a big fiddle leaf fig. Luckily, there are lots of plants that have healing powers (see page 152). Again, the same rules apply when thinking about the climate in your room. If it is big and bright, what about a palm? If it's hot and humid (what are you doing in there?), rainforest plants will thrive.

Blustering balconies
If your balcony is on the zillionth floor of a tower block, or your outdoor space is exposed to the whims of the weather, choose coastal plants that are used to being whipped by the wind. Seaside pinks can pack a punch while grasses will bend gracefully, adding foliage, texture and instant 'high flying' style. Or try bamboo, which has adapted long sturdy stems to stand tall against the elements.

GREEN UP YOUR WORKSPACE

Before I opened my florist I worked in recruitment. So trust me, I know what it's like to work in an office. Windows that don't open, ferocious air-con and dark cubicles may seem like a plant's worst nightmare, but actually the right plant will be perfectly happy here. And just like in the home, plants can breathe life into your working space, and literally make you better at your job! Even blaring out Mariah on Friday will sound better, as plants absorb background noise through their leaves and stems. Ooooooooh.

All bosses should get 'em in. There has been masses of research done on the subject of plants improving the working environment: they increase happiness and productivity, reduce sickness and absenteeism, and even just being able to see a plant from your desk can improve your concentration. So many companies pay for really expensive buildings and all the latest fancy gizmos, but is there any green in sight? No, Siree. If you've got an office space, big or small, think plants!

But, before we all go running to the florist on our lunch breaks, there are a few things to consider when becoming a plant boss. The same rules apply as when you are buying plants for you home, so what do we do? Let's go back to the roots...

Space, light, air and temperature are all factors when deciding what plants will be happy and where. Once you've discovered your desk is the perfect sunny spot, or you have the shelves to fit a spider, may your plant babies and pay-cheques grow big and healthy.

Desk buddies
Where? A desk that has access to bright light.
Who? The sun-lovin' succulent.
How? Let them join in payday drinks once a month.
Watch out! Make sure the sun isn't scorching your plant. Move if so.

Shelf sharers
Where? Those shelves that need a little spruce.
Who? The hanging spider plant.
How? They love a drink in summer and less in winter.
Watch out! These guys are pretty easy to hang out with. Just watch the watering.

Filing fillers

Where? On top of your filing cabinet.
Who? The easy-going devil's ivy.
How? They don't mind light or shade and like a drink once a week.
Watch out! Don't get those documents wet! Make sure you've got a pot without holes or a saucer underneath to catch any water.

Boss hiders

Where? Floor fillers to obstruct views!
Who? The big cheese, the cheese plant.
How? Always allow the soil to dry out between watering.
Watch out! That leaf might be nicely obstructing the boss's head, but remember to rotate the plant so all the leaves get equal access to light.

Floor stoppers

Where? The corners of rooms with bright but indirect light.
Who? The rubber tree plant.
How? Water once a week, and put this guy near the kettle so he can get a regular spritz whilst showing off to Julie from finance.
Watch out! Make sure wheelie chairs can roll round this guy so he doesn't get knocked.

Wait! Who waters the plants?

Right Plant Boss, you've got to make some rules here because cups of cold tea and a top-up every time someone goes to the water cooler can cause a cacti calamity. My advice? Water your own.

I love how the London photography studio, Clapton Tram, embraces a rainforest feel with all those lush ferns hanging from the ceiling!

ONE FOR THE WEEKEND:
THE GREAT OUTDOORS

Not having a garden shouldn't stop you from expanding your plant horizons from inside to out. Sure, you might not have a blade of grass or even a speck of soil, but has that stopped you from creating a plant paradise inside? When it comes to the great outdoors it's ALL about getting creative with your space. From the forgotten front door to passageway potentials, there is always room for a plant. Many people now live in shared spaces which gives room for communal gardening. Is there an abandoned planter outside your flat? Dig it! Space is scarce and we're claiming anything we can get our soily hands on.

The abandoned planter
It's big, concrete and filled with fag ends. But this is a potential wild wonderland. When approaching this as a microclimate, a planter that is shaded by the big building above it can be the perfect place for woodland plants to thrive. Think anemones, foxgloves, lady's mantles and ferns. But before we get carried away, first things first, who is going to look after it? If it's just you, you are going to want to keep things simple. Easy plant care is essential. Second, you're gonna want to get the most for your money, so go for plants that will give you interest all year round. Why not be ambitious with a crab apple tree? Beautiful blossom in spring, berries in autumn and apples to make jelly in winter... a total winner! The Evereste is my favourite variety of crab apple, as it is a small tree that won't get out of hand. If that sounds too pretty for your liking, try something more striking like pairing agapanthus with prostrate rosemary. Always go for the evergreen agapanthus as these will give you more variation, filling your planter with tall purple flowers through the summer months. Prostrate rosemary looks wicked, as it drapes itself over the sides of containers creating great heights and textures and it is still as tasty as its upright cousins.

Bloomin' balcony
There are so many options when it comes to crafting a secluded area where you feel fabulously enclosed by beautiful plants and able to sip on a glass of Shiraz, watering can in hand. The first question you need to ask yourself is what microclimate your space creates. Is it a sunny or shady? Windy or sheltered? Or patches of both? The answer to this question will narrow down the types of plants that will thrive in your elevated haven. Study how sunlight moves across the space over the course of a day and group your containers – sun lovers vs. woodland plants – in areas where they will thrive.

I suggest you invest in a large evergreen shrub (or as many as you can get away with in your allotted area) to create the base for your verdant paradise and add lots of different-sized plants to create layering, texture, scent and colour. Make sure you have a mixture of evergreen perennials and annuals to give an all-summer-long burst of colour. It really is worth investing in more established plants, too, as they offer immediate impact, but do mix in smaller plants among them – nothing beats the feeling of nurturing those babies and watching them grow. Vines and fast-growing climbers are good for a small space because they will create vertical interest in a short amount of time (jasmine is a highly scented winner and the bees love it).

Next up, over-the-balcony planters. There are so many great options out there, so fill them up with herbs and, if you're up high, coastal plants that will bend in the wind. Then put up some macramé hangers of varying heights to add interest from above. If you can't hang them from the ceiling, use a hanging basket bracket and hang them from there. When it comes to selecting pots, I get my inspiration from the Mediterranean – think brightly painted terracotta urns, patterned tiles, old vintage vessels... Keep a daily eye on your garden as container plants can dry out very quickly, and feed your plants once a month with an organic fertiliser.

Forgotten front doors
If your front door opens to the outside world you have planting potential! (Don't worry if you're in a hallway, you've got loads of houseplants options here too.) If the space is looking like it needs a lick of paint and the landlady is saving her coppers, why not smarten things up with a posh olive tree? These create instant style. Want to up the style ante? Try two either side of the door. Double posh. Avoid small pots, as these guys will just get in the way. You can add colour by under-planting your olives with seasonal plants such as bulbs in the spring, lavender in the summer and cyclamen in the winter. They are also great for hanging Christmas lights to get things feeling really festive. These guys like full sun and do like a good drink in the summer. Feed once a month and reduce watering in winter but don't allow the compost to dry out completely. A big problem for city dwellers is pesky plant thieves! Try running a chain through your drainage hole or securing it to the wall to keep it safe.

Passageway potentials
Passageways are usually gloomy places where the bins hang out, but they also offer plant possibilities. Rather than planting bushy shrubs that will grow outwards and get in the way, try climbers that can be trained to grow up walls. The climbing rose Zéphirine Drouhin will thrive here. It loves shade and can climb up to 3m, so it will go wild on the side of your building. It smells gorgeous and, most importantly, has no thorns, so you may find yourself making excuses to take out the rubbish.

The base of the wall is perfect for shade-loving plants like ferns and cyclamen, which will add a splash of colour in the dark. If your passageway is particularly narrow, try rectangular pots that will take up less space. If the passageway is long, place your pots two-thirds of the way down to break up the space.

Off the wall

Every wall has its own microclimate, from a south-facing suntrap for plants from the Med to a shady spot perfect for forest dwellers. Lots of walls brave the elements, so native coastal plants, which are used to more challenging conditions, may thrive there. South-facing walls call for sun-loving Mediterranean plants like lavender and herbs that will enjoy the heat – but don't forget those Europeans like a drink. East-facing walls are prone to frost and dramatic drops in temperature so go for hardy plants, such as forsythias, that have adapted to varied climates. Your north-facing wall is the perfect hangout for shade dwellers. Woodland plants like ferns and foxgloves will be particularly happy here and the white flowers of a winter jasmine will lighten up a dark corner. West-facing walls are usually protected from cold north winds and get good amounts of sun so many plants will be happy here; try roses and jasmine to add fragrance. When it comes to containers there are loads of options. For the wall itself use hanging baskets and wall mounters but triple, quadruple check they are secure. For climbers, use wire or a wooden trellis for plants to spread their leaves. If your wall isn't too high, try fixing a container to the top and trailing plants down. Mix it up and get creative – just make sure you have good access to look after them properly.

THE EXOTIC GARDENER
PAUL SPRACKLIN ~

When I first saw Paul on *Gardener's World*, I put down my glass of wine and said to myself, 'I have to meet this man'. A fellow Essexer and plant obsessive, we're soulmates! Paul is a true British gem – when everyone tells you you can't do something, what do you do? You bloody do it, don't you! Mad dogs and all that. So when everyone said he couldn't grow tropical plants in his garden, Paul created a jungle! And a massive one at that. Paul very kindly let me come and have a look, so I headed up the road to see for myself.

Sitting at Paul's table, I genuinely thought I saw a monkey climb up one of the palm trees, only to realise it was a squirrel. I was getting tropical fever already. Palms towered over us as succulents climbed the big slope that Paul has built for his, er, rock face! Paul has recreated the microclimates his plants need: open, sunny spaces for cacti, shaded, damp spots for ferns, a canopy of palms and even a homemade bog for carnivorous creatures. He likes to garden in 'communities', putting plants from all over the world who have the same requirements together, so they can get the same care. I especially love the umbrellas placed over the succulents so they don't get damp. A BIG shout out goes to his 6m cacti that is nearly as tall as his house! When I quizzed Paul on houseplants, he confessed to only having one, a hardy mother-law's tongue that gets very neglected compared with its cousins outdoors. We agreed you should probably aim to do one thing and do it well...

I love the introduction to your website: 'The imagery conjured up by this website is of an extremely exotic nature. Only continue if you are not of a nervous disposition or easily excited.' What is it about tropical plants that gets you so excited?
For me, there is something decadent about plants with strong form – architectural plants seem to make up a kind of fantasy landscape. A garden full of such plants is always, for me, reminiscent of hotter and more exotic lands and will generally put a smile on my face.

What is your experience of seeing these plants in their natural environments?
I've made a number of field trips to Mexico, travelling through the multitude of climate zones and habitats there, ranging from arid plains and temperate woodland to cloud forest and lush, wet tropical rainforest. But even in some of my more local favoured holiday destinations, such as the Canary Islands, there are wonderful natural sites to see. No time for beaches!

I read that some of your plants started life as houseplants, is this true?
Yes. That is how this whole exotic gardening thing started for me. Back in the mid '80s I had, for the first time, a small piece of outside space that I could call my own. Not knowing

any different I planted one of my ailing houseplants – a yellowing *Fatsia japonica* – and it thrived! That got me wondering what other plants that looked like houseplants could be grown outside and, subsequently, it has become an all-consuming passion. Some might say obsession.

How does your (exotic) garden grow?
Slowly, and with very little interference from me! I tend to grow my plants 'hard' – with very little extra irrigation or food – in the belief that they are better equipped to deal with adverse conditions when presented with them. Soft, nitrogen-bloated plants seem much more susceptible to pests and the cold. Perhaps that is simply my justification for being a lazy gardener!

As the 'flag carrier' for exotic gardening (Grace & Thorn salutes you!), what advice would you give indoor exotic gardeners?
Turn down the central heating and don't water them as often as you think you should. Also, invest in wider windowsills!

What is the secret to succulents?
Benign neglect.

Finally, I heard you had to get rid of a beloved Aloe vera houseplant. Tell me about your life together...
Ah, yes, poor Vera. Childhood sweethearts, she caught my eye when I was just a young man, staying by my side through life's ups and downs. Many times healing me when I was sick. But, sadly all too common, I started to take her for granted, didn't value her quiet dedication, and found my head being turned by younger and flashier plants. So it was, I left her outside one winter and she was taken from me. Filled with remorse, I vowed never to neglect any of my old favourites again.

PLANTS THROUGH
THE SEASONS

We all know the changing seasons affect plants outside, but what about plants inside? All plants have adapted to their environments to survive, but plants have been on this planet for millions of years. Central heating? About 60 years... So, as it stands, a plant will still change with the seasons, even in our homes.

When it comes to the change in seasons for houseplants, I like to look at the similarities between plants and people: a sense of renewal in spring, soaking up the summer sun, settling down in autumn and chilling out in winter. If you are watching your plant babies well, you will start to notice those behaviours. The most important change comes in the winter when your houseplant goes into a sort of hibernation, or as you and I might call it, they chill the fuck out after a busy year. This is when you get some time off, too, as watering, feeding and general care comes down to a minimum. And it's good for everyone to have a little rest before things start to hot up again in spring. Calendars out, here is a rough guide of what you can expect.

SPRING CLEAN

'Spring is here! I'm so excited I wet my plants.'
So, we've all had a great Christmas break, but it's time to get back on it. This is a great time to clean up your plant act. Give your plant babies a spring clean with a good haircut and wipe down big leaves. Spring is also a good time to repot your plants, as they are in their most active growing phase. By repotting you will stimulate new growth and give the plant plenty of room to grow. However, this doesn't mean you need to get all your plants changed, just choose the plants that need a new look or have outgrown their old one (see page 178 for more on repotting). The increase in temperature and light means your plant is going to start needing more water, too. Increase gradually and use the classic finger test (see page 202). The same goes for feed: little by little does the trick. On warm spring days, throw open the windows to give them some fresh air and humidity.

SUMMER, SUMMER, SUMMER TIME

Summer brings heat, humidity and happiness for most houseplants and, of course, lots of lovely light. Get your sun-lovin' plants a good suntan but watch out for those south-facing windows – the summer sun can get really strong and scorch your plants, especially through the glass. Summer is also a good time to give some of your plants a little holiday by sending them outdoors to revel in the fresh air, get a good clean from the rain and a healthy glow from the sun. But not all houseplants will be happy outside, so always go back to the roots to see who would prefer to stay at home. Also, remember that holiday-goers love a good drink and can often pick up an unwanted pest or two.

WINTER IS COMING

I love autumn. My houseplants are settling down at home, basking in the last of the sun and getting ready to settle in for winter. This is the time to bring holidaying plants back home before the first frost and give them a good check over to make sure there are no slugs hiding in their soily suitcase! The thing to watch out for in autumn is the central heating. Thermostats are turned up and air becomes too hot and dry for humid-loving houseplants. Keep an eye on these and get the misters out. This is also the time to help ease your houseplants into winter by slowing down on the amount of water and feed you give them.

IT'S CHRIIIIIIIIISTMAS

As the days get short and the nights get colder, your plants will like nothing more than settling down and cosying up in front of the TV. This is their dormant period when they stop growing to save energy for spring. Keep them happy by letting them be. Some plants watch their drink in winter, so reduce watering to just once a month. If you're a fan of whacking the heating up, you should give them a little more to drink but keep an eye on the soil – roots can get soggy and damp in winter as it's harder for them to dry off. Make sure you let the soil dry out completely before you water again. Sun-lovin' plants, like succulents, should be moved to rooms that get more light over the winter months and make sure tropical leaves don't touch the frosty windows. Forget haircuts at this time of year, as it will only encourage leggy growth as your plant isn't going to want to put in the effort. Now, settle back and pass the remote.

THE AGONY PLANT'S GUIDE TO BLOWING HOT AND COLD

How to deal with central heating

The reason many of us are lucky enough to live with houseplants is the fact that centrally heated homes can pull us out of Arctic conditions and place us somewhere our plants feel more at home. But, unlike the humidity of the tropics, radiators produce hot dry air, so forget plants that like humid conditions. As a rule of thumb, most houseplants aren't fans of fluxing temperatures so being right next to a radiator that is going on and off won't make them happy, although you could try succulents who are used to hot days and freezing nights in the desert.

It is also important to note the differences that the seasonal change will bring to your plant. Unlike us humans, these guys seriously cut back on the food and drink over Christmas, but when the heating is on full blast, they are going to start to get thirsty so you may need to top them up a bit.

How to deal with air-conditioning

Let's face it, on this side of the pond we don't have much call for air-conditioning in our gaffs, but if you do, it's important to understand its effects on your houseplants. Air-conditioning removes the humidity and heat that many houseplants crave, especially rainforest ones! They thrive on lovely humid, hot conditions — a no-no when air-conditioning is involved. Keep things humid by regularly misting leaves and watering soil.

If the colour of your plant's leaves is fading or if the leaves are wilting, it could be because the plant is too close to an air-conditioning vent. Cold air blowing directly on to plants strips away their moisture. Choose plants that can cope with variations in temperature and humidity. Tough guy yucca will deal with almost anything the air-conditioner throws at him. As a general rule, plants with large leaves can normally cope with a little puff now and then — think palms and mother-in-law's tongue. Terrariums are also great for protecting plants from the effects of your air-conditioner. If all else fails, turn it off and sweat it out!

KEEP IT GREEN.

The Agony Plant
xoxo

Avoca-do.
Avoca-don't.

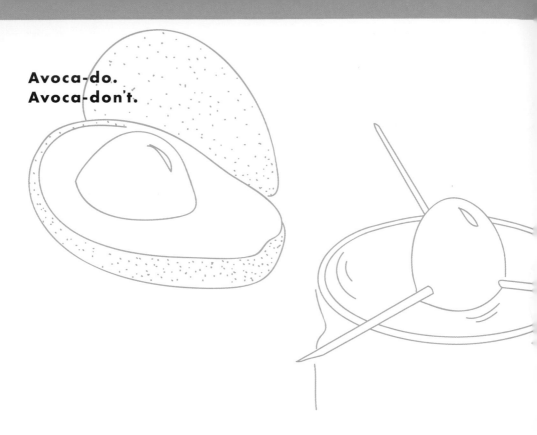

There is nothing more rewarding than growing plants, only to be able to eat them, too! Growing your own requires more time and dedication than you give to your houseplants and you will need to call the plant babysitter if you're planning a holiday, but these guys can be pretty unfussy once you get them going. You can even grow lots of things from leftovers! Growing your own is an easy and inexpensive way to live. And live well.

First, let's talk about the avocado. Yes, it goes with everything. Yes, it looks great on Instagram, but have you read about the deforestation the demand is causing? Now, I'm not saying you should stop eating them (breakfast would never be the same!) but maybe this is your chance to do some good and grow your own. OK, it may take 10 years for an actual fruit to grow, but it's a start!

How to grow your own avocado plant

Lot of people say you can't grow avocados in the UK, but to them we say guac off! The three sitting in my kitchen window aren't complaining. Going back to the roots, these guys usually flourish in the sunshine states of the Americas, so give your plant as much light as possible by placing your jar on a sunny windowsill. Growing your own avocado is so easy to do and a great thing to show off to your friends. As I said, it may take up to 10 years for it to seed fruit, but what's the rush? Now, pass the nachos.

A STEP-BY-STEP GUIDE

1. Eat a delicious breakfast (poached eggs on avocado toast, if you're asking).
2. Save the avocado seed and clean off the leftover green mush.
3. Work out which is the top (sprout) and bottom (root). As a rule, the bottom is flat.
4. Spear the stone with cocktail sticks to create outstretched arms and legs.
5. Suspend the stone over a glass of water with the bottom half submerged.
6. Place your jar on sunny windowsill.
7. Change the water once a week to keep it clean.
8. Wait.
9. Wait a bit more.
10. Crack! The stone splits. The roots will start to grow in the water and a stem will reach for light.
11. When the stem has reached around 15cm, pot it into soil.
12. Look after your avocado plant baby and let the 10-year countdown commence!

How not to kill your avocado tree

Avocados need to be kept moist but not soaked, so make sure it has good drainage. If all else fails, do the finger test (see page 202). You'll know if you are over watering as the leaves will start to wilt and turn yellow. Feed once a month in the summer but keep an eye out for white crust on the soil – this generally means a build-up of salt from the fertiliser. If you spot it, flush the pot out by rinsing it thoroughly, let it drain and then repeat. Every spring, repot it into a larger pot to help it grow strong and healthy. For the first few years, give it a haircut to create a big bushy plant but the first serious trimming should happen only when the plant is around 30cm tall: cut it back to 15cm to allow for new leaves and stems to grow.

If you like piña coladas?

How to grow your own pineapple
Thanks to their popularity on Pinterest, pineapples have been enjoying a bit of an 'it' moment and I bet you have a few hanging around your gaff. HALT! Before you spot one that's outstayed its welcome, pineapples are super easy to regrow. All you need is a glass, water and those all-important cocktail sticks. A great excuse for another party. Piña colada, anyone?

STEP 1. EAT

Take the freshest-looking pineapple you can find, slice off the the leaves – leaving the stem intact – and devour said pineapple. Finely slice into the stem, until you see a ring of brownish dots – these are your roots! Don't worry about cutting the fruit off, it will only go mouldy so get rid.

STEP 2. DRY

Pull off some of the lower leaves to expose the stem and help it sprout roots. Strip away until 6–8cm of the stem is exposed and make sure to cut away any remaining fruit. Leave to dry out for about a week – this is important as these guys can rot easily. You'll see when it's dry because the scars where you cut into it will harden.

STEP 3. SOAK

Find a glass that can house your pineapple. Try to find one that is a little on the small side so your pineapple can wedge in it and not be submerged. Fill with water. Now, poke a cocktail stick (there should be some leftover from your avocado plant) into both sides of the pineapple so it can be supported by the rim of the glass. Lower it into the water, submerging the stem, keeping the leaves dry.

STEP 4. ROOT

Place the glass on a sunny windowsill and wait for the roots to sprout. In a few weeks you should spot little white roots poking through! Change the water every few days to prevent it going mouldy and try to keep temperatures consistent.

STEP 5. POT

When the roots are 10–15cm long, you're ready to pot your pineapple! Prepare a pot with good drainage (these guys are fond of cactus soil), push the roots in and press around the soil firmly. As it continues to grow, you will need to repot it into bigger pots to stop it getting root-bound.

STEP 6. CARE

Your pineapple should be easy to grow if you apply the same rules as for your other houseplants. It needs a sunny, warm and humid environment, and try to keep temperatures consistent. Definitely don't let it freeze. Water once a week at the most, and mist regularly.

STEP 7. EAT?

Hold up. Depending on where you live, it may take a while for this pineapple to pop out. You're also going to have to wait until it reaches at least 60cm. Try and be patient and be proud of helping this little fruitless fella into the world.

You say tomato.
I say tomato.

How to grow your own tomatoes
Tomatoes. Who doesn't love them? A lot of people, weirdly! However, they are in my top five foods along with corn on the cob. And they are so easy to grow. Whether you have an outside space or not, the humble tomato will be happy. This is my partner Tom's favourite plant project. In the summer our home is filled with bowls brimming with deliciously different shaped and sized tomatoes. I love the wonkiness of the real deal. From orange to black, the colours are varied and while some are perfectly round, others are oblong, bulbous and beautiful. Who wants rows of identical tomatoes? How boring! And the taste! Nothing tastes quite like one of your own. Sweet and peppery, and bursting with flavour. Be prepared to create vats of delicious tomato sauce or to be typing 'tomato recipes' into the internet. A favourite of mine comes from Nigel Slater: you simply bake the tomatoes with garlic and pour over a dressing of olive oil, anchovies and basil. Yum. Some people go off-piste: I have a friend who adds tomatoes to her Marmite on toast.

I love watching my tomatoes grow from seed, but you will also find lots of small plants on offer. These are also fine, but just check the plant is happy and healthy before you take it home (see page 136).

118

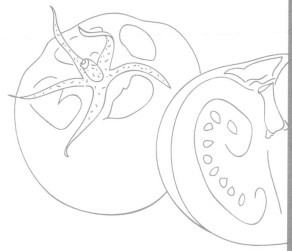

HOW TO GROW TOMATOES FROM SEED

STEP 1. HUMBLE BEGINNINGS
If you are growing your tomatoes indoors, look out for the 'vine' varieties. The first phase is sowing your seeds – any time from February. You will need a small pot (empty yoghurt pots work a treat) and good potting soil. Wet the soil, create little holes and pop a small handful of seeds in each. Cover the hole with soil and water. Voila! You are ready to grow.

STEP 2. FIND THE PERFECT SPOT
OK, time to go back to the roots. Tomatoes are native to South America and Central America so we know they like lots of sunshine – position them on a sunny windowsill. Your plant will take about a week to appear. Water every day to help them grow big and strong and remember to rotate them so they grow straight and tall.

STEP 3. A NEW HOME
Once your seeds have sprouted a few leaves, they're ready to go into a bigger pot. One about 15cm wide will be perfect. Carefully tip them out of their current home and give their roots a little tickle. Transfer them into a new pot filled with soil and give them a big drink.

STEP 4. GROWING UP
The most important thing with tomatoes is to watch the watering. These guys hate drying out. It is also important to feed them with a good fertiliser every few weeks. Once they start to get tall enough, they will need some support. Insert a cane into the soil and loosely tie the stem of the plant to it with twine.

STEP 5. GROWING PAINS
Your tomato plant may be so happy that it grows too big. Check for 'suckers' – vines that start to grow in between the main stems – and pinch them off with your fingers. Outdoors, bees and insects will help the plant pollinate. Indoors, when flowers begin to bloom, give Mother Nature a hand by tapping the stem with your finger to move the pollen around the plant.

STEP 6. LET'S EAT
Your tomato plant should now be growing big and strong. If you're lucky enough to have a greenhouse or outside space, move your plant there. If not, just keep making sure they are getting enough light and water. When the fruit starts to appear (around August time), ripe ones will twist off easily in your hand.

THE PLANT CHEF
TOMOS PARRY ~

Being part Italian, food is a very important part of my life. Luckily for me, Hackney, the home of my first shop, has a wicked food scene – even our local has a Michelin star! A Portuguese deli has just opened next door. Custard tart? Yes, please! We've even got a local farm that grows some of the ingredients it then cooks up in its tiny restaurant. My mate Tomos was head chef at nearby Climpson's Arch before he jet-setted down to central London to open Kitty Fisher's, where he now serves Brad Pitt! I LOVE Tomos's cooking, especially his use of plants and flowers – his fried sage gnocchi is a must-try. Recipe coming up. You're welcome. We met up to discuss all things plants and food.

How do plants feature in your cooking?
I often use them to elevate dishes when particular plants are in season. For example, I try and use the flowers of the plant or vegetable that is in the dish, as they will generally be a lot more fragrant that the plant or vegetable itself, so it adds another level to the eating.

Have you ever worked with flowers and food?
Using flowers in cooking became very fashionable a few years ago, but I first experienced it at the River Café in Hammersmith. They had their own garden, where, before service, I would collect all the flowers and fresh herbs to use as garnish. My favourite dish there was sea bass carpaccio with tomato and many types of fresh herbs and beautiful flowers torn over it. I also worked at Noma in Denmark, which has a very disciplined 'locally sourced' approach to cuisine. The chefs there forage the flowers themselves and everything they use in their dishes has to grow in the area. So, for example, because citrus does not grow natively in Denmark, they use wood sorrel for acidity, and for black pepper they use Nasturtium to add pepperiness to dishes. All very inspirational.

Can you describe how 'seasonal produce' relates to the plants you use?
I will only use flowers and plants if they are in season. The simplicity of my cooking style relies on my understanding of seasonality and using the plants and produce at their peak. Using plants should feel natural to the dish, instead of using it just for the sake of it. Wild garlic is one the highlights of the year for me: I love using the leaves for cooking and as a garnish, and seasoning with the wild garlic flowers at the end.

Have you seen any trends with plants in the world of professional cooking?
Yes, mainly driven by the Nordic food scene, which René Redzepi and Noma started in Copenhagen. I would say that Noma and Nordic food have created a revolution in food. There are many reasons for this, but I would say that their use of plants and locally foraged flowers and herbs would be the main aspect of their very inspirational and ground-breaking approach.

What is the most unusual plant you've cooked with?
Pineapple weed! This is a wild herb, which I used to forage in London Fields and make syrups with it while I worked at Climpson's Arch. It's a small yellow bud that grows with grass (*Matricaria discoidea*, but commonly known as pineapple weed or wild chamomile). It's very common and everyone will have seen it. If you pick it up and rub it, it will smell so strongly of pineapple. At Noma we used to forage kilos of it then infuse it into sugar syrup. People could not believe that this vivid pineapple flavour came from a common wild weed.

Do you grow your own edible plants at home? If so, what are they and what are your tips?
It's quite tricky in my one-bedroom flat, and with my long hours I feel like I can't give enough time to keep them alive! I do grow some, but they are robust herbs such as thyme and rosemary, as they can look after themselves! I usually steal bay leaves from my neighbour's overhanging tree.

Can you give us any tips for cooking with herbs?
To get the most out of any herb, use when you start cooking and then use the same

amount at the end. Herbs develop in flavour and lose their aroma, so at the beginning of the cooking they will add the depth, but it's the essential to add the exact same amount of herbs right at the end, when the dish has come off the heat, as this will bring the dish alive with the natural aromas!

Please can you share your famous fried sage recipe ☺

FRIED GNOCCHI, SAGE, BROWN BUTTER, BLACK PEPPER AND BERWICK EDGE

* 1kg russet potatoes (or any high-starch potato), cleaned
* 150g plain flour
* 2 teaspoons salt
* 1 egg, lightly beaten
* rapeseed oil
* 4 tablespoons room-temperature unsalted butter, cut into small pieces
* 20 sage leaves
* 1 teaspoon lemon juice
* freshly ground black pepper
* 60g Berwick Edge cheese, finely grated (Berwick Edge is a strong Gouda-like English cheese, very similar to Parmesan)

Cook the potatoes in the oven at 160°C until tender (around 45 minutes). If you can pierce them easily with the tip of a knife, you're good to go. Remove from the oven and, as soon as the potatoes are cool enough to handle (letting them cool will also help the mixture go gummy), peel and pass them through a potato ricer into a large bowl.

Sprinkle the flour and salt over the potatoes and, using your hands, make a well in the centre. Pour the beaten egg into the well and stir in with a wooden spoon. Turn out the dough onto a floured surface and gently knead for about 2 minutes, dusting with more flour as needed, until smooth but not elastic (be careful not to overwork it). Divide the dough into 8 pieces. Roll each piece into a 60cm-long rope about 1.5cm thick. Then cut into 1.5cm pieces.

Bring a pan of salted water to the boil, throw in the gnocchi and blanch until they float. As soon as they float (around 2 minutes) take them out with a slotted spoon, toss in oil and spread on a tray to cool in the fridge.

Melt the butter in a pan with all the sage leaves, and turn up the heat gradually. The sage with start to crisp and the butter begin to brown. Once the butter is a light brown colour, take it off the heat and add the lemon juice. Leave to one side.

When the gnocchi have cooled, warm a frying pan with oil over a medium heat and carefully fry the gnocchi for around 1 minute on each side until golden brown. Now add the butter and sage to the frying pan, season very well with black pepper, and serve with the Berwick Edge.

Finally, what's Brad Pitt like?
Brad is pretty chilled. I mean I don't see him that often, ha! But when he and Bradley Cooper came to the restaurant, Brad took down a whole Galician beef rib-eye himself (which is meant for two people to share), so I think he likes his meat. He also bought a very nice bottle of wine from our list, of which he only had one glass, and gave the rest to the kitchen because he enjoyed the food so much.

HOW TO CULTIVATE A CHIC INDOOR HERB GARDEN IN SEVEN STEPS

There's nothing like opening your favourite cookbook, knowing you already have all the herbs you need to cook dinner within the sanctuary of your kitchen. Such is the beauty of growing your own indoor herb garden, which is simple, satisfying and easy to nurture throughout the seasons — not to mention delicious and cheap, too! Save supermarket herbs by dividing them up for your own herb garden (see page 215). These guys will have been squished into a tiny pot, so set them free! Here's my seven step guide to creating the perfect herb garden.

Step 1: Let there be light
A sunny kitchen windowsill is ideal for your indoor herb garden. Make sure it gets at least five hours of bright light a day, as a lack of sunshine will leave you with stressed plants that lose their flavour. If you don't have a windowsill, look for other spaces in your house that get a lot of sunshine. Remember, you can always use macramé hangers if you don't have much space.

Step 2: Is it hot in here?
Indoor herbs like the same temperatures that most people do —

so if you're happy, they probably are as well. These guys aren't too fussed about the temperature dropping at night either, just make sure the foliage doesn't touch the glass in your windows to protect them from getting chilly.

Step 3: Choose your herbs wisely
When it comes to selecting herbs, follow your palate. I take my inspiration from my Italian grandparents, so basil, sage and parsley are a must. Chives make everything taste better and have you ever ruffled a bushy thyme only to have the whole room smelling sweet five seconds later? Bliss. Herbs can be divided into hard and soft. Soft herbs are basil, chives, mint — these are delicate, so they need a little more care and attention. Hard herbs, such as thyme, rosemary and sage can cope with less water and light.

Step 4: Pick your pots
Open the cupboard and look at your plates. If you're matchy-matchy you might want something sleek and uniform, but if you've got more of a mismatched thing going on, try combining different pieces to create variety. Check out eBay, charity shops and car boot sales — just make sure the pots are porous and have good drainage. You will also need a saucer under each pot to catch water and protect your surface — again, look for the pieces that match your personality.

Step 5: Pot your herbs
Start with something to help drainage at the bottom of your pot (perhaps smash up that chipped plate that's been bugging you and use a few pieces!), then place a small mound of potting soil in the pot for your plant to sit on and water it thoroughly. Carefully remove the herb from its original pot and gently loosen the roots with your fingers. Position the herb on the soil mound and check it from all sides to make sure it's centred and sitting up tall and straight. Add potting soil around the herb, pressing it down with your fingers until firm. Now give it a big drink to help it settle down.

Step 6: Time for a drink?
If the surface of the soil feels dry, you need to water it. Give them a good drink until water fills into the saucer, but be careful not to over water them — herbs don't like to sit around in wet soil. For extra tasty herbs, feed your plants once a month.

Step 7: E voilà! Dinner is served
Once your plants are 15cm tall, snip away! Don't be shy: the more you use, the bushier they'll become. Try not to trim more than one-third of the plant's foliage at a time though, as it will get stressed. For tall herbs (think chives) snip 5—8cm off the top. For more bushy herbs (think parsley) you can cut entire stems from the outside of the plant as the new growth will fill in the space.

KEEP IT GREEN.

The Agony Plant
xoxo

Rating
Easy peasy.

Name check
Look at the hanging leaves and think tails.
I then think of the sunny Mexican climate
it comes from, which makes me think of
a donkey walking across the desert – a
donkey named Burro!

The deets
This guy is all about texture: thick, lush
leaves from a braided plait. Very on trend.
Show it off by hanging it on your balcony,
but remember this guy gets pretty heavy
so make sure the pot is sturdy enough to
support him. It will lose its leaves – don't
worry, it happens.

Back to the roots
Burro's tail is a hanging succulent,
hailing from the warm suns of Mexico. So
everything we've learnt about desert plants
applies here. First things first: watch the
watering. This guy hates being wet. Second,
he needs light but sunburns easily, so watch
those south-facing windows in summer.
Feed once a month. If any bugs appear, just
give it a good shower (and see page 209).

How not to kill your burro's tail
Clever succulents store water in their
leaves. If he's thirsty they will start to
shrivel so give him a drink but wait for the
soil to completely dry out before you give
him another. He'll let you know if he's not
getting enough light by going weak and he
won't grow.

BURRO'S TAIL *Sedum morganianum*

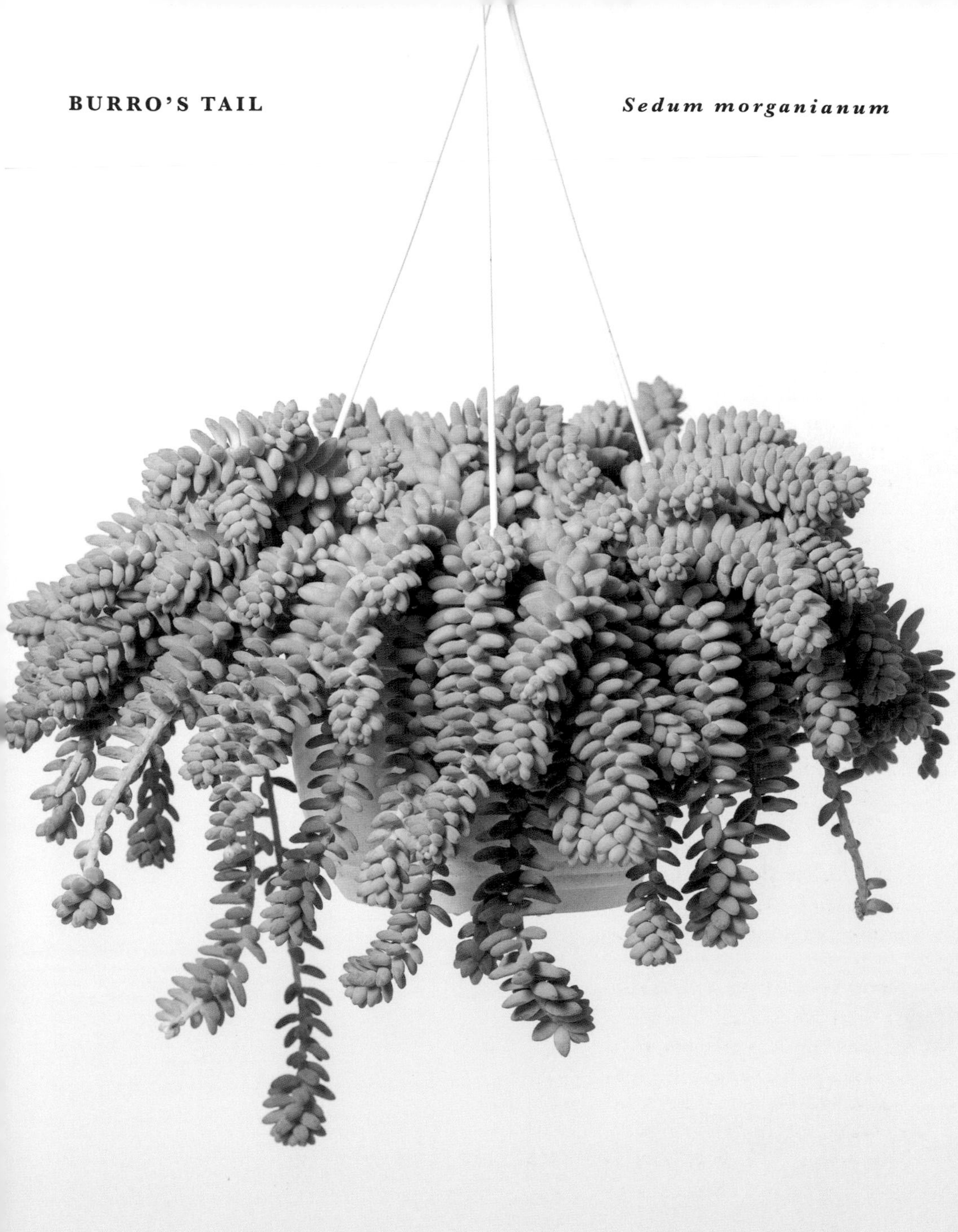

STARTING A

2

PLANT FAMILY

A GUIDE TO
BUYING PLANTS

It's no secret that I'm obsessed with plants. Big, small, rude looking, it doesn't matter. I love 'em all. I find the whole experience of owning them so soothing and therapeutic, as well as rewarding, and I get such a kick out of seeing how obsessed our customers also become! I watch them grow, look after them when they're poorly and show them off to everyone on Instagram. So when people come into the shop, I want them to find the perfect match to start a plant family of their own.

As I hope you will have already learnt from reading this book, you can't just plonk a plant anywhere, so first I ask prospective parents what kind of space they have. Is there lots of light or it shady? Do they have a lovely humid bathroom or sunny south-facing windowsills? Once we know this, then we can look at the plants that will thrive there (see chapter 1). Second, I ask them, realistically, how much time they have to commit to plant parenting. There is no point in fibbing. Even if you've got no time, there's a plant for that. Some houseplants are almost indestructible, while others are a little more needy. Choose the ones that you know you can be there for. Now you know what you can provide for your new plant babies, which ones are you going to choose? This is where the fun starts!

What the florist?!

I would *always* recommend you buy your plants and flowers from a florist. Oi! I can see you rolling your eyes going, 'Oh yeah...?'. But it's true! Only florists will spend time with you, teaching you about the plant and making sure it's the right one to take home. I love talking with my customers about their plant's needs and putting different plants together so they can see what they could look like in their gaff. You can also be sure that your prospective plant baby will be strong, healthy and void of disease or pests. AND you can also pick up the perfect pot, stock up on soil or choose a fancy new feed to look after it at the same time. Compared with supermarkets or shopping online, you will get a personal service at a florist where you can ask all your questions, arming you with all the tools to start a healthy and happy plant family.

Unexpected plant guests

We all buy our plants from Grace & Thorn (obvs) but what happens when you go to the supermarket and they're suddenly selling succulents, or your nan gives you a new collection of spider plant babies? Taking home the wrong plant is not only wasteful but can often impact your other plants back at the ranch through unseen infections. First things first, always think about the plant's roots (where it's come from) and whether you can recreate that climate back at home... Got the perfect spot? Here are a few things to consider when shopping elsewhere:

Supermarkets
Poor supermarket plants. Squashed and squished into cellophane, kept in dark storage rooms, under watered and then left in a centrally heated warehouse right next to the draft of the sliding front doors. If there is anyone who hates supermarkets, it's plants. Supermarkets tend to sell disposable plants. Florists (should) sell you plants for life. If you're reading this and fancy yourself a supermarket plant saviour, you might be in for some hard work – these guys will be suffering from serious supermarket shock. If you don't have the time, I wouldn't bother.

IKEA
Lots of people buy plants from IKEA, and they live very happily together. As far as I can see, IKEA stock the easy-going guys that are pretty tough, so success rates are high. But there is a word of warning I want to give: they don't name their plants. This is the most important thing about your plant baby – without its name you won't know how you should look after it.

Flower market
Flower markets are a great place to pick up cheap, healthy plants. But remember, a lot of flower markets are going to be getting rid of old stock so you need to know what to look for. Avoid plants that have lots of open blooms; they may look pretty now but they'll be over much sooner. Also, think about how you're going to take your new plant home. Is shoving it into an old plastic bag doing it any favours?

Nan's gaff
So, your nan is trying to offload her spider plant babies onto you? Before you say yes (and you know you have to say yes!), have you got somewhere with light to grow them? Luckily, spider plants are as easy as nan's apple pie recipe, but if it's something more stubborn or tricky, maybe think twice before you obviously say yes. Check the plant is healthy and happy and there are no signs of disease or stress.

Online
The biggest issue with buying plants online is that you won't be able to check them for any signs of trouble. At Grace & Thorn we sell houseplants online, but as with any good florist you can trust we'll send you a healthy specimen. A lot of problems can also happen in transit if your plants aren't packed properly. If you're buying from a bulk store that doesn't specialise in plants, it's likely the poor thing is going to turn up looking a little worse for wear and may go into shock. Good florists will transport their flowers well so they turn up ready to settle in immediately.

How to pick your perfect plant partner

When it comes to selecting the best plant from the plant pack, it all comes down to your personal taste, but here are a few things to look out for when you're looking for love.

If it's all about looks
Upright, bushy, trailing, climbing or rude? Houseplants come in all shapes and sizes. But don't overlook plants that are a bit wonky. Wonky is most definitely sexy. And it's important to remember that those pretty petite succulents may look cute now, but they can grow into bulbous- looking <insert rude word here> in no time. Fit.

Does size really matter?
People are often intimidated by how big plants can get. But, remember, it doesn't happen overnight or even over a few years! In most cases, you can trim back where necessary if it's getting out of control. I say embrace it. All you need to make sure you can provide is the right amount of light and the air to help it grow. If space runs out, you can always move your plant somewhere else or trail it around pictures and windows. I think bigger is most definitely better.

Are you a commitment phobe?
I have been asked on at least five occasions, 'How long will my plant last?'. Plants are for life, not just for Christmas! Most tropical plants can long outlive their owners so be prepared to go in for the long haul. Just imagine it, you, your grandchildren and that rude-looking cactus all hanging out in 2050!

If you struggle to keep the spark alive
If you get bored easily, remember, it's not all about green. Houseplants can fill your home with colour, too. Have you ever seen the neon pink vein on a fittonia? Look for leaves with multi-coloured spots and stripes or be surprised by a flowering cactus.

Swipe left or right
Like all new flatmates, it's important to check them out before they move in. Sadly, you can't spy on a potential plant's Instagram feed, but there are a few things you can look out for to know whether this one is going to be suitable:

YES
Strong, healthy-looking leaves
A bold, vibrant colour
Sturdy stems
Unopened buds

NO
Curled, withered leaves
Discoloured or pale
Insects or larvae
Space between the soil and side of the pot
Furry mould on base
Roots growing out of the pot

IT'S A MATCH!

Going home together
I love nothing more than seeing someone carefully cradling their new houseplant baby home. But don't forget that before that point, most likely it will have lived a sheltered life in a greenhouse, and then been lovingly pampered in the florist's window. As soon as you both walk out the door, it's in for a shock. Make the process a little easier by carefully wrapping the plant to protect its leaves and keep its temperature consistent.

NAME CHECK

I'm terrible with most names, but I always make sure I learn what my plants are called! It's just practice, and whether you stick a name tag on it, repeat it 20 times or go to bed with a massive houseplant encyclopaedia, do it! Not only will it make you look super-pro when friends come round, it's imperative for looking after your plants. As soon as something goes wrong, you can look it up. Hopefully, you will have placed your new plant away from your pooch's paws but, if the need arises, you'll also need to know what your furry friend has eaten for a quick recovery. With each of the plants in this book I have provided a little tip to help you remember its name. This is the start of a beautiful relationship between you and your new plant babies and by living with them, you will get to know them even better! By watching them grow, you will learn what they need, and the best thing is, plants give back too (see page 151).

Shop rejects

One man's plant trash is another man's plant treasure
I am always amazed at the plants that get overlooked in the shop. Sure the big
fiddle leaf fig tree is waving its big sexy leaves at you, but make sure it doesn't
bedazzle you away from the little spotted begonia over in the corner. The same
happens when certain plants are 'on trend'. Pfft. I don't go in for that. I often take
the plant rejects home to look after them and watch them blossom. So don't fall
for trends. Choose the plants that make you happy.

BEEN SPOTTED BEGONIA

Spotted begonia
Begonia x corallina

Rating
Super chill.

Name check
There are over 2,000 types of begonia, but the foliage types can be recognised by their patterned leaves. You can't not love the spotted variety, so remember the spots and remember them well.

The deets
I remember begonia peeking through my nan's cheese plants. This now makes sense to me, as begonia began life on the rainforest floor, where only slivers of sunlight could trickle through the canopy above. Scientists have recently discovered that the begonia's wild cousin, who still lives there, the *Begonia pavonina*, has evolved almost luminescent blue leaves to help them survive in the darkness. Even more amazingly, it actually *slows down* the speed of light to get more energy from it. No wonder these guys are so adaptable! Begonia is a big deal in Italy, but the one in my shop didn't sell for six months, so I took him home. What an unusual, attractive plant to have and one that always reminds me of family and holidays. *Saluti!*

Back to the roots
Most of the begonias we have in our homes today are adaptations of their cousins from the rainforest floor, but their roots hold true, so don't place them on a south-facing windowsill but rather somewhere they can get bright but indirect light. They love warmth so make sure they are away from draughts and they hate being soggy – so watch the drink! Once a week should do the trick. These guys are pretty pest resistant, but try to keep their leaves dry to avoid problems, although they love a good mist – and feed – once a month. When it starts looking unruly, give your begonia baby a haircut to keep it neat and tidy and to help it grow big and strong. Each spring, move your begonia baby to a bigger pot – make sure there is good drainage.

Blooming lovely
If it's really happy, your begonia may produce beautiful white, orange, pink and red blooms. If you really want them, keep an extra eye on feeding and make sure it's getting plenty of light.

What's wrong with my spotted begonia?
If the leaves are wilting, you're either over or under watering. A process of elimination will get you back on the right path. If it's not growing, check the light and watch the drink. It may also have become pot-bound so move it to a bigger pot.

FIT-TONIA

Fittonia
Fittonia verschaffeltii

Rating
Fusspot.

Name check
This plant is sure to catch you eye – think, 'they're fit' and then take it home with you as soon as possible.

The deets
This sexy devil has deep-green leaves covered in a distinctive vein pattern in bright white, pink or red (I have a huge crush on the pink ones), but these designs aren't just for show. Fittonia have adapted to live happily on the dark rainforest floor, where the colour in the leaves traps what little light it can get down there. Fit and clever, you say? Back off, guys, I saw it first! To keep it looking so good takes some work though – it doesn't like dry air, draughts or direct sun. But if you're up for the challenge, it's most definitely worth it.

Back to the roots
This handsome creature is native to the tropical rainforests of South America, and mainly Peru. It grows as a ground cover and can grow over 30cm, making it perfect for low-lying terrarium texture. This tropical treat will thrive with the help of high humidity, so make sure to mist it every morning to provide the moist air that it craves. Or place the pot on a tray of wet pebbles to increase humidity around the plant (see page 210). Starting life on the rainforest floor means it needs indirect or dappled sunlight and will burn easily, so keep it out of the glare. It can be pretty damp down there on the rainforest floor so keep the soil moist but don't let it get soggy.

How not to kill your fittonia
Watch the watering. Fittonias will collapse if they dry out and its leaves will go limp and yellow if it gets too soggy. Their soft stems and leaves easily attract fungus, gnats and mealy bugs, so keep an eye out for pest raiders. This guy is ALL about the foliage, so pinch off any small flowers that develop as they will weaken the growth of the leaves.

HUNKY BEEFSTEAK PLANT

Beefsteak plant
Iresine herbstii

Rating
No beef with this one.

Name check
Also known as bloodleaf (red leaves) and chicken-gizzard (say, what?!). Quite a few plants share the common name 'beefsteak', so it's easy to misjudge it. Do not confuse with the begonia variety.

The deets
Everyone wants green! I had a maroon variety in my shop and nobody touched it. So I took it home, put a picture of it on Instagram and everyone went wild for it. This plant is all about colour. Bright shades of red and purple leaves with prominent red veins. POW! Imagine that colour popping in your gaff. It's nice for leaves to get a shout out over their petally cousins once in a while, too. Small flowers may appear in summer but you can pinch them off if you want, because they aren't nearly as stunning as the fabulous foliage. Because of their tropical tendencies, these guys make excellent bathroom partners, so maybe consider a toothbrush to match!

Back to the roots
From Brazil, this tropical tearaway needs warmth, humidity and lots of light. It also likes lots to drink so water thoroughly, aiming to keep the potting mix moist at all times. It's easier to pot these guys into pots with drainage, so you can remove excess water and prevent soggy bottoms. Bloodleaf plants need less water in winter, but never allow the soil to dry out completely. The more light it gets, the stronger its colour, so top up its tan near a sunny windowsill – but make sure it doesn't get sunburnt in direct rays. When it comes to temperature, these guys like to be warm so keep away from draughts and keep the mister to hand. They will be very happy in a bathroom where the humidity and heat levels are high.

What's wrong with my beefsteak?
If it becomes leggy or pale, it isn't getting enough light. Watch out for aphids – these tiny pests love the soft, new growth.

Rating
Not so easy peasy.

Name check
Beautiful little rows of pearls (or peas) hang
off its string, like a necklace. Fancy.

The deets
This is one of our bestsellers, but also one
that I struggle to keep alive. A good friend –
who confesses to having killed lots of plants
in her lifetime – has the most beautiful
string of pearls that lives in her window. I'm
always trying to get tips from her, but she
swears she doesn't do anything! All I can
take from this is that it loves light and a bit
of neglect. I'll keep trying. There's no doubt
it looks striking – the pearls sprawl over the
sides of the pot and it looks great hanging
from a macramé hanger or windowsill.

Back to the roots
First, it's a succulent so watch the watering.
Too much and it goes mushy and mouldy.
Remember, these desert plants survive long
periods without any water at all. In fact,
their clever pearl-like balls store water,
which means you can water thoroughly
one week and then pretty much forget the
next week or two. Water even less in winter.
Like most succulents, these guys love bright
light. Giving your string of pearls a haircut
to keep it nice and tidy is easy to do: just
trim off any dead stems, and any stems that
have lost a lot of their beads.

How not to kill your string of pearls
Even though it is pretty relaxed when it
comes to drought, it does not like being cold.
You'll know if it's feeling chilly because
the leaves drop off! Make sure that the
temperature isn't ever less than 7°C.

All the gear and no idea!

I can't choose who I love more, Monty Don or Nigel Slater. You? Either way, I love a man who knows how to use a fork. But, unlike the outdoor gardener, the houseplant owner does not need loads of tools to keep their gaff green. Sometimes a kitchen spoon (or fork) will do the job. Keep your tools in one place so they're easy to access – I use a big wicker basket with handles.

Soil
Good old potting soil is great for most houseplants while soggy-bottom-hating succulents need a special cactus soil, as it's fab for drainage. See page 196.

Drainage
Drainage is the Holy Grail for houseplants, especially if you're using pots without holes. Without drainage the water won't be able to drain and your roots will rot. See page 167.

Feed
When it comes to feed, it is important to give your plant baby the nutrients it needs. Read the menu on page 198.

Water
Tap, bottled or rainwater? Some houseplants have a discerning taste when it comes to their favourite tipple. Find out more on page 202.

Watering can
Watering can? Watering can't? Can, we say. Some plants hate having wet leaves (I'm looking at you, begonia), so opt for small nozzles and long spouts.

Trowel
Oh, so useful for repotting and moving soil. Here you can go fancy and opt for a Japanese design. I love the Niwaki range – beautifully crafted and they last. But, like I said, a spoon will do the job too.

Mister
We LOVE misters. You can get some seriously fancy ones or just keep it cheap by washing out an old cleaning spray... and label really well! Keep next to your plants for easy access.

Damp cloth
Useful for keeping leaves clean. Any old thing will do. Make sure it stays away from the cleaning cupboard so it doesn't get any chemicals on it that could harm your plants.

Scissors
For haircuts and cutting off wonky bits. Good plant scissors will give a cleaner cut meaning open wounds are less susceptible to infection.

Newspaper
Business section? Nah, you're alright. Keep unread bits of *The Sunday Times* for mess-free repotting. Also useful for handling cacti!

Pots
I like collecting pots to dress up new babies or give old ones a fresh look. The pot chapter (pages 160–191) will introduce you to some of G&T's signature styles. Dinosaur, anyone?

Pan and brush
Sounds so obvs, but oh, so useful.

Milk
A wise nonna once said that milk was great for cleaning leaves. She wasn't wrong.

THE AGONY PLANT'S GUIDE TO PLANTS, PETS AND BABIES

As the owner of three wild whippets, I can confidently say my plants and pets live happily side by side. But, as any pet owner will know, vet bills can be massive so prevention is better than cure. If you are a cautious cat or dog owner, there are lots of houseplants that are non-toxic so you can have guaranteed harmony in the home. But if, like me, you're plant-obsessed, at the end of the day it all comes down to common sense — don't plonk toxic plants next to their watering bowl! We already proof our homes for our pooches with gates and guards so the same rules apply with your plants. I always recommend keeping your plant babies out of reach of little paws. If you start to see nibbles, move your plant somewhere your pets can't get to.

If you come home to find your pet has feasted on your foliage and is looking a little worse for wear, take them to the vet immediately. It's a good reason to learn all your plant names so you don't have to lug the plant there with you. By knowing what plant it is, you can help the vet find the cure.

Online, the ASPCA (American Society for the Prevention of Cruelty to Animals) has an extensive list of reported problems. Below, I have included the plants in this book of both toxic and non-toxic natures (luckily, lots of our favourites are in the latter group). If you have a plant that isn't in here — use the website as a guide.

When it comes to kids, the same rules apply — keep the plants off the floor! Whenever kids come into my shop they seem instantly drawn to the spikiest cacti in there! As mum is busy flirting with Mr. Fig Tree, I watch as their little one gets closer and closer, but as the hand reaches out, mum always picks them up. Instinct!

TOXIC

Aloe vera
Patients: Toxic to cats and dogs
Symptoms: Vomiting, diarrhoea, tremors, change in urine colour
What to do: Call your vet immediately

Asparagus fern
Patients: Toxic to cats and dogs
Symptoms: Excessive itching and grooming, rashes, sneezing and watery eyes
What to do: Call your vet immediately

continued overleaf...

Jade plant
Patients: Toxic to cats and dogs
Symptoms: Nausea
What to do: Call your vet immediately

Mint
Patients: Toxic to cats and dogs
Symptoms: Nausea, vomiting, diarrhoea
What to do: Call your vet immediately

Mother-in-law's tongue
Patients: Toxic to cats and dogs
Symptoms: Nausea, vomiting, diarrhoea
What to do: Call your vet immediately

Philodendron
Patients: Toxic to cats and dogs
Symptoms: Irritation of tongue, mouth and lips, difficulty breathing
What to do: Call your vet immediately

Scented geranium
Patients: Toxic to cats and dogs, but cats are more sensitive
Symptoms: Diarrhoea
What to do: Call your vet immediately

Swiss cheese plant
Patients: Toxic to cats and dogs
Symptoms: Irritation of tongue, mouth and lips, difficulty breathing
What to do: Call your vet immediately

Tomato plant
Patients: Toxic to cats and dogs
Symptoms: Hyper-salivation, severe gastro upset
What to do: Call your vet immediately

NON-TOXIC
Avocado tree (except if you live with horses…)
Basil
Begonia
Boston fern
Burro's tail
Haworthia
Parlour palm
Rubber plant
Spider plant
Thyme

The Agony Plant
xoxo

PLANTS WITH BENEFITS

Plants and flowers literally breathe life into our homes, connecting us to the great outdoors even in the middle of the concrete city. They are symbols of love, of thanks, and of 'shit, I forgot!'. It's not just a physical connection either – we green up our Instagram feeds until our scrolls bloom, keeping Mother Nature close to hand wherever we may be. At Grace & Thorn we think Plants = Powerful. They boast pollutant-busting powers, work their magic on detoxing our mood and can up a room's style ante, all at the same time. Amazing.

Now for the science bit. Concentrate...
Believe it or not, people used to think plants could harm you in the home. This led to loads of scientific studies providing evidence that plants *definitely* benefit people. One of the most famous is NASA's 1980s study on air quality in sealed environments, natch. They proved, categorically, that leaves and roots help remove 'toxic vapours' from inside contained spaces. Leading the space race were low-maintenance Boston ferns and rubber plants, clever things. Recently, plants have been found to tackle chemicals in cleaning products and can even combat nail varnish! Next time you go for a pedi, check if the salon has houseplants, as they've been proven to reduce acetone levels by 95 per cent. They'll even help reduce your chance of getting a cold because they increase humidity and decrease dust.

Play nice, be clever and give plants as gifts
Did you know that your obsession with plants actually makes you a nicer person? Really! Research shows that people who hang out with plants tend to have better relationships because plants increase our feelings of compassion and empathy. A recent study also found that flowers can benefit our mood and emotions (see over the page for more on this). They have even been found to boost memory! The same study suggests people who give plants and flowers as gifts are more likeable, friendly and emotionally intelligent. Right on!

Superstitious? Nah, us neither.
Next time you go for a Chinese, check if there's a money tree (jade plant) for prosperity and good luck. Legend goes, a poor hardworking farmer came across an unusual little plant. It was stubborn and hard to uproot, but he managed to bring it home. It was resilient and didn't need much care to grow, so he took a lesson from the plant – be stubborn and resilient, too. And you know what? He became a great entrepreneur. The moral of this story? Be more plant, people! Have you ever had a mystery waft of basil? This tasty herb is seen as a sacred plant, used to protect the home and its occupants. Superstition goes that souls of good people smell of basil.

Pop a plant pill

When you're feeling a little under the weather, nervous about a date or can't concentrate at work, turn to plants. They have been proven to help in all these situations. Don't eat them, whatever you do, just put them in your home and let them work their magic. All you need to do is give them a little love in return.

Feeling anxious?
What will help? Spider plant.
Why? People who keep plants and flowers in their home feel happier, less stressed and more relaxed. The spider plant is the perfect option. A low-maintenance foliage feature requiring little light and able to survive a less-than-reliable watering technique. These are virtually kill-resistant, so let go of those worries and see your mood soar as your plant-nurturing works wonders.

Feeling distracted?
What will help? Parlour palms.
Why? It's scientific fact that houseplants increase productivity and memory retention. The calming influence of nature increases a person's ability to concentrate on the task at hand. Forget sparse minimalism, a green abundance will increase oxygen and leave you happier and more psychologically engaged. Go big with a palm that will keep a strict eye on regulating humidity and reducing carbon dioxide in your home.

Feeling blue?
What will help? Yellow ranunculus.
Why? Yellow is the best colour to create enthusiasm and can awaken your confidence and optimism. Bring back the sunshine and seek out strong pops of yellow in your home. Sunflowers may be out of season, but that's no reason to forget the power of buzzing colours. The super-brights of the ranunculus

make a perfect, multi-tasking purchase: guilt-free, functional blooms with serious swagger.

Feeling sleepy?
What will help? Mother-in-law's tongue.
Why? Studies have shown that having plants in the bedroom can lead to a more restful sleep. And, although she might not sound it, mother-in-law's tongue is perfect for tucking you in at night. Instead of taking in carbon dioxide and turning it to oxygen during the day, mother-in-law's tongue is one of only a few plants that releases oxygen at *night*, making it the perfect plant to have in your bedroom, cleaning the air as you sleep.

Feeling poorly?
What will help? Rubber tree plant.
Why? Dry air and dust can irritate your senses. The microclimate around plants increases air humidity and reduces dust in the home by up to 20 per cent, therefore reducing the effects of a runny nose, sore eyes and sensitive throat. A rubber plant not only cleans the air and reduces dust, but it battles germs, too, by killing them while they're airborne. This process does not harm people or pets, but it can reduce the bacteria in a room by as much as 50 or 60 per cent.

Feeling uninspired?
What will help? Swiss cheese plant.
Why? From Matisse to Hockney, cheese plants have found their way into the homes of our

favourite artists. Not only does the lure of the tropics fill the imagination with dreams of tigers and lions and bears, plants are proven to increase creativity by 45 per cent!

Forest bathing

Fancy getting outside to heal? Why not try the Japanese practice of 'forest bathing'? It is, quite literally, spending time in a forest, soaking up the atmosphere, and it has been scientifically proven to boost your health. Japanese officials spent $4 million(!) dollars studying the effects of forest bathing, measuring the activity of cells in the immune system before and after exposure to the trees. The studies showed significant increases in cell activity in the week after a forest visit, and positive effects lasted a month. Why? It was due to essential oils in the forest air, emitted by the trees to protect themselves from germs and insects. Forest air doesn't just feel good, it will actually improve your immune system.

Plants have feelings, too!

My partner often finds me in the sitting room nattering away to our fig tree or in the bath catching up with the fern. Have I finally lost the plot? No!

I love the film *The Secret Life of Plants*, not just because Stevie Wonder does the soundtrack, but because it attempts to prove that plants have emotions. This idea of 'plant perception' – where plants can feel – is widely dismissed because plants don't have a nervous system, but there is *loads* of research that proves it may actually be true!

Many people believe plants are 'conscious' in how they react to their surroundings. For example, scientists discovered that certain plants release an oil to repel munching caterpillars. When they played the sound of a caterpillar to the plant (with no caterpillar in sight), it still released the oil, meaning plants can hear! Sort of. Plants have memories, too. Another scientist set up an experiment with the mimosa plant, which curls up when it senses danger. They dropped the plant on the floor, and what happened? The leaves curled. But as they began to repeat this process, the plant learnt that nothing bad was going to happen so it saved its energy and stopped curling. When they dropped the plant a month later, it still remembered.

One of my favourite experiments was done by Dorothy Retallack who published a small book called *The Sound of Music and Plants* in 1973. She filled two rooms with plants. In one she played rock music and in the other, soothing tones. After five days she noticed dramatic changes in the plants. In the soothing room, the plants were super-healthy and even bending towards the radio. In the rock room, the blooms were dropping and bent away from the speakers. By the end of two weeks, the relaxed plants were lush, green and happy while the rock 'n' roll plants had lived fast and died young. Sorry, Lemmy.

MARIE'S MEDICINES
MARIE BAXTER ~

The Town Hall Hotel is up the road from my Hackney shop and I can often be found in there, searching for a Bloody Mary, or hanging out with the manager, Marie, and her greyhound, Dizzy. We've collaborated on loads of brilliant things together from our Jungle is Massive display at the hotel, to their alternative Christmas tree, not to mention a wedding or 20. Marie casually told me she used her Aloe vera plant in her smoothies. Wicked! I caught up with her, and Dizzy, in her amazing oak-panelled office at the hotel to find out more.

How did you discover uses for the Aloe vera?
My work in hospitality took me from Ireland out to Indonesia. They grow fields of Aloe vera over there and the roads are filled with little shacks where you pull over and buy Aloe vera drinks, which are great for hydration. I'd never dreamt of using it back in Ireland, but I learnt that you can use it for everything from sunburn to cuts. So, when I came back to the UK, I asked the people who do the plants in the Town Hall Hotel to get me the biggest Aloe vera plants they could find. They thought I was mad. 'What? Why do you want to do that?'. When they saw that I was using it, people started giving me the plants as gifts (I am told I am not easy to buy for!).

Why did you start putting it into smoothies?
I don't drink milk, so I started drinking Aloe vera gel as it is full of calcium. It's also great for healthy digestion. I wouldn't drink it every day though – maybe three or four smoothies a week.

Yum! What does it taste like?
Tart. I really recommend you don't eat it raw – I can taste it now!

Please can I have your signature smoothie recipe?
Fill the blender and blitz:
* Aloe vera gel – one stalk does the trick, skinned, of course
* Coconut milk – a good glug
* Frozen fruit – whatever you are in the mood for – I like mango or raspberries
* Ice

Which part of the plant can you use?
Only the gel. You have to be careful because there is poison in the skin, so make sure you cut it properly. It's like filleting a fish; once you get the hang of it, it's easy.

How do you look after your Aloe vera?
I keep them in big pots at home. In the mild weather they go outside and in the winter, especially if there is frost, I bring them in. I water them very little, as they rot if you over water. A pint once a week seems to do the trick. They grow babies phenomenally fast in the summer – the babies will eat the mother so you have to pull them out pretty quickly!

Any other tips for those who want to try it?
I've learnt all this from doing it, but it really is easy – just don't eat the skin, don't drink it too often and don't forget to snip off the babies.

Sounds like you have green fingers!
I could actually kill a cactus fairly easily. It is purely for selfish reasons I grow plants – if I can't eat it, I won't grow it. Aloe vera plants really don't take much looking after though. I did start growing rhubarb after I saw it being sold for £1 a stalk in the supermarket! I thought, 'You are having a laugh – back in Ireland it's a weed!'. I went and bought some from the garden centre and now it has taken over 15 per cent of my garden! I bring it in for the staff at the hotel who make everything from rhubarb jam to rhubarb vodka!

I love Dizzy, tell me more about her...
Dizzy is a greyhound and she lives here as the hotel dog. She is a rescue dog and only has four teeth left, poor thing. She is very insecure and follows me around everywhere! The guests and staff love her. I thought I might get a few complaints because not everyone likes dogs, but it has never happened. Instead, we have guests who request to sleep on the same floor as her and brides who want her in their photo shoots – she has a better social life than me!

ALOE VERA *Barbadensis*

Rating

The plant that can do it all, so you have to do very little.

Name check

Say 'aloe whenever you pass a plant with big juicy leaves that grow in a spiral from the inside of the plant.

The deets

Over the years, the Aloe plant has made quite a name for itself and is probably rather smug at this point. The 'do it all' plant soothes burnt skin, heals cuts and can be found in lots of people's fridges, cleansing our bodies and souls in liquid form. It doesn't stop there though, as this plant helps clear the air of pollutants found in our everyday chemical cleaning products. Apparently, you will see brown spots starting to emerge on the leaves if an excessive amount of harmful chemicals is present in the air. Now, I think that deserves a gold star! Our own personal nuclear alarm. Known to the Egyptians as the plant of immortality and to Native Americans as the wand of heaven, this plant can seriously do it all! Aside from being an excellent body cleanser, Aloe can also help indigestion, upset stomachs and ulcers. It also alleviates joint inflammation, making it a great option for arthritis sufferers. One study found that gargling Aloe vera juice was just as good at removing plaque as mouthwash – a brilliant chemical-free alternative.

Back to the roots

This succulent hails from Africa so it loves to be in the sun (though they will tolerate some hours of shade) and do well in dry climates. There are hundreds of varieties, ranging in size from tiny weeny to as tall as a tree of 9–12m. They also come in many colours including orange and pink and their textures and shapes can vary dramatically, too. Unlike other succulents, they are extremely susceptible to frost so make sure they are well protected from the cold in winter. These guys are tolerant of dry conditions but they still love a drink. Give them a good soak but always allow them to dry out in between.

How not to kill your Aloe

If the leaves start dropping or are becoming almost transparent, your plant is either thirsty or has had too much to drink. Ask yourself when you last watered your plant? If you watered it recently, it's time to admit it to the houseplant hospital and check for root rot. If the leaves of your Aloe vera plant are turning brown or red, your plant may be getting sunburned. Remove these leaves at the base with a sharp blade.

How do I harvest Aloe vera?

If you already have a happy-looking Aloe plant, all you have to do is lop off a mature leaf, slice it open lengthwise and scoop out the gel. Be careful as the skin contains poison.

POT

3

LUCK

CONFESSIONS OF
A POT HEAD

On top of the fridge, placed onto shelves, next to the TV, at the edge of the bath, hanging from curtain rails, on every windowsill in the house... wherever there is a space, I put a plant in it! I love plants in mismatched pots and holders. You can often find me raiding charity shops, buying from eBay and seeking out vintage shops for odd bits and pieces. I have plants in copper pots, handmade ceramics, collected Beswick vases, hanging in macramé, flowers in old milk bottles and lots and lots of handmade pottery. Saucers make wicked dishes for pots with holes, and you'll even find a cactus in the matching teacup. When my mum comes round she always says, 'God, this is just like your nonna's house'. I guess she's right. It's rammed full of plants and antiques, not to mention the packets of pasta in the cupboards and an espresso-maker, or two.

When I started Grace & Thorn, I saw a gap in the market – no one was making houseplants look desirable! They were all crammed together in boring brown plastic pots. How many poor plants are left to live a boring, cramped life in the plastic pot they were brought in? Not only will your plant probably have outgrown its first home, but this is your chance to reflect your style and make it your own. That said, if you've just brought it home, it's a good idea to let your new plant settle in first, so wait a few weeks before you get creative. But when you're confident your plant baby is happy, it's time to up the style ante. Be original! We all love classic white, but what about a ceramic giraffe?! Having always been obsessed with ceramics, I am happy to say my shops are now overflowing with some bloody amazing pieces. Colour, style, texture and shape are all important factors when choosing the right pot for your plants. And if you get a little bored of an old plant, you can dress it up in something fancy.

How to find your perfect pot

Plastic fantastic
Who? The lazy gardener.
Why? Plastic pots are affordable, lightweight and won't break when your puss knocks them over. But if your plant is getting massive, get it out of there. Plastic pots are far less stable and more likely to wobble than their sturdy terracotta cousins. Plastic does not absorb water like clay, so your plants will need less watering. But, honestly, they look naff. Give your plant baby something special to show off in.

Terracotta army
Who? The classic gardener.
Why? There is something refined about a good terracotta pot and they certainly get better with age. You can pick up terracotta pots pretty cheaply from garden centres and the great thing is you can easily paint them to suit the style you want. Think cool Mediterranean whites and blues. They are also great for big plants to stop them toppling over. Remember that they are porous though, which means they lose water more easily than their plastic cousins – you just need to remember to water a little more often.

Bold as brass
Who? The magpie gardener.
Why? This is understated bling, for someone who can't resist a bit of glint and shine.

Cool as copper
Who? The boss gardener – cool, sharp and hard to please.
Why? Win extra kudos at work with your impeccable design credentials. It's totally on-trend – calmly poised and ready to impress.

Little China girl
Who? The fancy gardener.
Why? It's a modern classic – but with an unusual edge. China and porcelain make excellent containers but don't go drilling into Aunt Beryl's set to make drainage; pebbles at the base will do just fine (see page 167). Classy aqua tones and interesting sculptural detailing shout timeless design.

Tin tins
Who? The sweet-toothed gardener.
Why? Who doesn't love a sneaky spoon of golden syrup just to get to the end of that tin? From advertising slogans to French medical tins, scour junk yards to find the perfect unique pieces – just make sure you've washed them well first.

Concrete slabs
Who? The urban gardener.
Why? So androgynous chic. Concrete and plants make a great pair: the sharp edges show off the soft textures of leaves. We are very inspired by the brutalist architecture at The Barbican Centre.

Original pot gangster
Who? The too-cool-for-school gardener.
Why? From animal heads to alphabet letters, you can be totally original with a bespoke piece. It can get addictive sourcing new pots... and be warned: it's far too hard to choose one from a set, so you may just have to get the whole collection. I also adore and own lots of ceramics – there is something very pleasing about owning something handcrafted by someone so lovingly, and they come in so many patterns and colours.

A hole in one

The first question you're probably going to ask is, 'Does my pot need a hole in it?'. Good question. All plants need drainage and many will argue that you have to have holes for your plant to thrive. But in my shop, I use pots without holes and my plants are happy. The secret? Good drainage. I like to use a gravel base when I pot up a plant, as this allows the water to drain well and the roots to stay happy. It is also useful for rented properties where you have to keep an extra eye on the furniture because it is less likely to leak. If your landlord is very particular or you're swagged down with antiques, add a layer of felt to the bottom of the base for extra protection. Simply cut the felt to fit and glue on to the base of the pot. As always, watch your plant. You'll soon see if it's not draining well, as the soil will stay damp and your plant will start to look miserable. Repot and see how it gets on.

Rating
As easy as ordering Chinese.

Name check
This is as close as you are going to get to
growing money on trees. Their large, round,
leathery leaves look like coins on the end of
a long, thin, succulent-like stem. Cha-ching!

The deets
The pilea started life as a houseplant
through the love of amateur gardeners who
spread it hand-to-hand via cuttings. Now
you can get pilea from most florists, but it's
important to give a little nod to those pilea
plant parents who made them available to
all. The pilea is not a fan of direct sunlight.
Mine love a spot in front of a window,
where they get a lot light, but nothing direct.
They're pretty happy in shade, too, but the
leaves might turn a darker green – pilea
parent's choice. Remember to let your
pilea practise its pirouette by turning the
pot regularly, allowing sunlight to reach
all sides. They get thirsty, so when you
give them a drink, make sure that you
completely drench the soil but let it dry
before you water it again.

Back to the roots
Native to China (obvs) and not a big fusspot,
just make sure they aren't in direct
sunlight, and they don't like it too hot.

How not to kill your Chinese money plant
If their lower leaves are dropping, it means
you are giving them too much to drink. In
this case, also make sure that the soil is
draining well. These guys also hate getting
too hot, so don't put them near radiators.

THE CERAMICIST
JESS JOSS ~

As soon as I saw Jess's work I loved it. Simple, classic designs with a wicked modern twist. I can't get enough of them in my shop and, as they are all made by hand, no two pieces are ever the same. She makes ceramics and nature look like they've always belonged together! Jess also does workshops to help others get their pottery fix. Another plant obsessive, I interviewed her to find out how she combines her two (or should we say three) passions.

How did you get hooked on pottery?
I've never really been not into it. My parents are potters, so I grew up in the pottery studio spending summer holidays helping out/ getting in the way. My earliest memory of working with clay is making clay pizzas with my sister. We would roll out a disc of clay and 'decorate' it with mushroom and cheese, all made from clay. Thankfully, these pieces were never fired. I was lucky enough that my school had a kiln so I could incorporate ceramics into my GCSE art. After completing an A level and degree in ceramics, I've never looked back. To gain more practical experience, I assisted other ceramicists before setting up my studio.

What inspires you?
For me, the holy trinity is cooking, gardening and pottery. Those are the three things that make me happiest, either in the kitchen, the garden or the studio. My inspiration comes from the time that I spend in these places. For example, at the moment I'm working on some ceramic hanging planters. I want to bring some of the plants from my patio indoors for winter but I've run out of space!

Amazing! Tell me more.
The new hanging planters will be relatively small and compact, with the pot 15cm tall and wide. I'm using leather cord to hang them through holes made in the clay. This year I attended one of your macramé planter workshops. It was great to learn a new craft and I'm hoping to incorporate some of the knotting techniques I learnt into the design.

Has your love for plants and flowers influenced your work?
They influence me daily. If I wasn't a potter, I would definitely be a florist. My plant pots and vases aren't only for decoration but to highlight the beauty of what they contain.

Do you make pots with specific plants or flowers in mind?
It's more the other way around. I like to make pots with varied surfaces, a few speckles or drips. Then I look out for plants that also have something a little different about them – an interesting pattern on the leaf or a strong shape to the plant.

What's the secret to holding a cool ceramics class?
I teach the way I would like to be taught – a lot of encouragement, demonstrations are key and a good laugh. You gotta laugh when things go wrong. Learning to use the potter's wheel can be challenging, but despite that, with even just a little practice, everyone can make pots. Making what you want to make is the hard bit.

If someone wants to make their own pots, where should they start?
Find a class. Google local potteries or your local college and see who offers workshops near you. Then be prepared to practise. Be patient and voilà... beautiful handmade pots!

What's your top tip for choosing the right pot for your plant?
I would offer the same advice as I tell my students when choosing a glaze for your pots. Have a think about the colours in your home and choose something similar on a pot. If it's for your garden, don't be afraid of a little colour – it can really brighten up your day.

Finally, palm or petal?
Petals forever. I once made a series of plates for an exhibition in Kensington Palace and each plate had a pressed flower petal design covering the front and back. It was painstaking work as each one was cut out and applied individually, but totally worth it.

PAINTED POTS
JARDIN MAJORELLE ~

If you are looking for inspiration for painting pots, search for the
Jardin Majorelle, Marrakesh. Designed by the French painter,
Jacques Majorelle, in 1919, these gardens are all about bringing
out the best in plants by using colour. Majorelle painted the
building, gates and awnings of the botanical garden in brilliant
and bold primary colours. Filled with palms, cacti and asparagus
ferns (to name a few) his pots were his pièce de résistance,
painted in bright lemon, orange and blue to accentuate the green
of the leaves and make them sing. 'Majorelle Blue' became his
signature colour – an intense cobalt blue that is said to 'evoke
Africa'. After his death in 1962, the garden was abandoned until
the fashion designer, Yves Saint Laurent faithfully restored it.

PAINT YOUR POTS, MAJORELLE-STYLE.

Evoke Africa in your gaff by painting your pots, Majorelle-style. It's time to get your craft on.

Step 1. Source it
First of all, source a variety of terracotta pots. These can be bought from Grace & Thorn (of course), eBay (great for random shapes) and from most garden centres.

Step 2. Prep it
Remove any price tags and stickers from your pot by soaking it in warm water, then scrubbing it with a stiff brush. Allow the pot to dry completely – it will take about a day.

Step. 3 Sand it
Lightly sand the outside of the pot with sandpaper, and then wipe the dust away with a clean damp cloth. Leave to dry fully. Sanding it will create a little texture, which will help the paint stick.

Step. 4 Seal it
You can use any waterproof finish for the acrylic sealer, be it matt, satin or gloss. Spray the inside of the pot with your chosen sealant, leaving it to dry between coats. Two to three coats should do the trick.

Step 5. Prime it
Applying a primer will help you achieve a smoother finish and prevent the pot from soaking up any paint. Hold your can of primer 15–20cm away from the surface of the pot and apply a light, even coat. You can apply a second coat, if necessary, but let the first one dry before you do.

Step 6. Paint it
I'm going to recommend an acrylic spray paint here, as I am all for a quick but efficient method! Hold the can 15–20cm away from the pot's surface and spray on a light, even coat. Allow this coat to dry before applying another. This can take anywhere from a speedy 15 minutes to a few hours, depending on the manufacturer's recommendations.

Step 7. Show it
After you are happy with the colour, get your plants out, and get planting! Aim for lots of different plants, varying in shape, texture and height. (See pages 181–183.)

Grace & Thorn potting service: the potting shed kitchen

Sooner or later, repotting houseplants becomes something you have to do to enable your plant baby to grow big and healthy. Plants should be moved into larger vessels as they grow up. Unless more space is provided for the plant's roots, they can become pot-bound. That is, the roots of the plant become cramped and form a tightly packed mass that inhibits growth. And sometimes you may just want to repot for a fresh look. I often do this when my plant babies need a little spruce up (don't we all?).

Any good houseplant book will teach you to repot your plants, but many fail to mention where this (often) messy process happens if you live in a one-bed flat with just enough room to swing a cat!

My inspiration for a 'potting shed kitchen' comes from my nonna and grandpa, whose house was so full to the brim with plants, outside and in, that they used their kitchen to do all their potting. There is something very personal about changing plants inside. The smell of fresh soil, shelves lined with pots and watering cans on standby. And the kitchen gives you easy access to water (although a bathroom can happily perform the same job).

The best time to repot is when multiple pots need changing at the same time – this way you can calculate how much soil you'll need and can tidy up in one swoop. I like to set aside a lazy Sunday for repotting. I put on some Billie Holiday, pour myself a Bloody Mary and spend the afternoon hanging out with my plant babies. Bliss.

First, you're going to need a table. Clear the table and cover it with old newspapers. Keep your bag of tools close to hand. You are going to need a trowel (or spoon) for soil manoeuvres, scissors to trim the roots, a watering can to serve drinks and, obviously, a bag of soil.

Table and newspaper? Check.
Soil, fresh pots and tools? Check.
Plant babies needing a new home? Check.
Bloody Mary? Check.

Then, we're ready to repot...

THE AGONY PLANT'S GUIDE TO REPOTTING

When to repot

If your plant has just come home from the shop, let it adjust to its new environment for a couple weeks before repotting. Plants are in shock until they get used to their new light, temperature and humidity conditions.

Young, actively growing houseplants should be moved into slightly larger pots with fresh potting mix once a year. Large houseplants or slow-growing plants can be repotted every two years or when they seem to outgrow their pots or look top-heavy. If a plant is thriving, you can assume it's happy.

Check out the scale! Does your plant look like it's going to topple over? Can you see roots on the surface of the soil or emerging from the drainage hole? Also, if the growth of the plant has slowed down or looks sad, these are all signs it's time for action!

It's a good idea to repot a plant at the beginning of a period of active growth, usually in spring. Repotting houseplants that bloom in winter should be done in early autumn, after their dormant period.

Here's a step-by-step guide:

1. Water plant

Lightly water your plant to help the root ball and soil slide more easily out of the pot.

2. Remove plant

Remove your plant from the pot by carefully turning it on its side, then support the main stem in one hand and use the other hand to gently pull the pot away. Try not to pull on the stem — if necessary, you can gently tap the pot on the counter, or use a knife or trowel to loosen the soil around the edges of the pot. Be careful not to yank it out or break the main stems of the plant.

3. Prune roots

When moving your plant to a larger pot, begin by inspecting the roots and soil. If the soil is in good shape, try to disturb as little of it as possible. If it's rotten or mouldy, shake away some of the excess, but remember that removing soil will stress your plant even more. If the roots are tightly coiled, use your fingers or a sharp knife to loosen or gently slice them so they can spread out, trimming away any really long ends. Cut away any rotten or dead roots. If you are repotting in the same pot, shake off the excess soil, then use scissors to prune back up to a quarter of the roots. This will help rejuvenate your plant while keeping it small enough to stay in the same pot.

4. Clean pot

Wash the pot with hot soapy water to get rid of any disease-causing microorganisms and insect larvae. Pat dry.

5. Add drainage

This is especially important if your pot has no holes (see page 167), but all houseplants will benefit from a good drainage layer in the bottom of their pot, as it stops the soil from clogging together and getting soggy — a big no-no for happy houseplants. If the soil you are using drains well though, it's not necessary to put gravel in the bottom of the pot.

6. Add soil

Make a small mound of soil in the pot for your plant to sit on. Measure the height of your plant and pot, and make sure the top of the root ball is at least 1.5cm below the rim of the pot, so that it won't overflow when you water it.

7. Position plant

Place the plant in the pot and settle it on the mound of soil. Look at it from all sides to make sure it is centred and sitting up nice and straight.

8. Fill pot

Add potting soil around the plant in layers, pressing it down with your fingers until firm. Don't bury your plant deeper than it was before — the leaves need light.

9. Water plant

Water your newly potted plant well, until the water runs out the bottom of the pot (if it has a hole in it, otherwise just make sure it's really well watered all the way to the base). I like to sit the plant in the sink or bathtub and give it a good drink, making sure the soil gets evenly moist while the excess water drains away (again, this obviously only applies to pots with holes). This is also a good time to spritz or wipe down the foliage to remove any dust and potting soil.

10. Settle it

Sometimes after watering, it's necessary to add a little more soil to fill in any low spots.

11. Trim plant

Cut off any dead or broken stems and leaves. If needed, lightly prune your plant to encourage branching.

GOOD LUCK AND KEEP IT GREEN.

The Agony Plant
xoxo

STYLING YOUR PLANTS: DOES MY CHEESE PLANT LOOK BIG IN THIS?

When it comes to styling plants, I take my inspiration from nature. Just look out the window – nature isn't sitting neatly side by side. It's got that, 'Oh this? I just threw it together' look. And it looks wicked. Grace & Thorn styling is all about asymmetry, odd numbers and breaking the rules. Instead of looking at floral designs, I look at art and fashion to come up with ideas. I like to think, perhaps a little grandly, that putting houseplants together is a bit like a fashion house creating 'a collection'. Things arranged together actually stand out alone. So forget about matchy-matchy; I want to see miss-matchy – I'm a maximalist. I know it looks good on Instagram, but I am so bored of seeing everything on white. Plants really suit pink. Use colour. Clash it. Mash it up. Foliage has so many wicked textures, from feathery to waxy and all the weird and wonderful ones in between. You can literally drape your home with rich, luxurious leaves just asking to be stroked (and don't forget a prick or two!). And don't get me started on patterns: graphic, bold, stripy, zig-zag. Mix these up as well. Forget luxury handbags, no one plant is ever the same!

Show-off

I love a show-off. Nothing can beat a big statement piece in a room. Choose plants that love being the centre of attention like the fiddle leaf fig. Keep it looking good with a haircut and groom now and then (see page 198). This will also help it grow big and strong. The bigger, the better, I say.

Get the family together

Plants look good together. Mix and match textures, shapes and colours to draw the eye. Little-leafed plants can stand up next to their bigger cousins. If you're a busy plant parent, you'll want to put plants with the same watering needs in the same place – that way you can regulate the drink. Hanging out together can also raise the temperature – perfect for humid-loving plants who like to get hot and bothered.

Be an odd ball

I am a bit OCD about even numbers! I think it always looks better to use odd numbers when grouping the gang together. Most designers will suggest a group of three, but I say, what about a group of thirty-three?! As long as they're all getting enough light, keep inviting them over.

Hang out

Trailing plants always look really impressive. When my plants grow long, I love to trail them around shelves, windowsills and door frames. If they need something to hold on to, twist wire around nails to create a structure and set them free!

Get high

Uneven heights look wicked in a display. Source old chairs, benches or shelves to keep different pots on different levels. Or what about using the ceiling, too? Hanging stuff above a display of pots – from a macramé hanger or pinning air plants up a wall – can create a real jungle scene.

Go wild

Just when you think you've gone wild, go 100 per cent wilder. When we do displays in the shop, we go big or we go home. Of course, it's up to you though; this is about reflecting your style. But I am sure you've got space for a little dinosaur in there.

#SHELFIE HOW TO ARRANGE YOUR POTS ON A SHELF

Shelves? I love 'em. Not only do they make wicked displays but they mean more room for plants. Win-win! You can't beat arranging wild, unruly nature over clean geometric design, but in my shop I've also been experimenting with old branches and bits of wood, putting nature on nature, to create a real jungle feel. Moving my plants around on the shelf is therapy for me. I love how you can make it look different every time by changing things up and swapping things about. It's such an impactful and inexpensive way to change the look of a room – each plant and pot combo has its own personality.

Step 1. Find a location
Walls are a whole lotta unused space ready for plant action! The first question to ask is: what kind of climate are your shelves located in? A sitting room sun-catcher, shady corner at the back of a bedroom or a humid hotbed in the bathroom? If your shelves are already fixed, then you let them dictate the plants that will be happy there. If you're putting up new shelves, make sure they are well secured, as that plant collection might get massive.

Step 2. Get the gang round
Once you know what climate your shelves are in, choose your plant gang accordingly. Bright light will be great for a cacti collection, while ferns will love hanging out in a humid bathroom. Shelves are the perfect place for trailing plants, like string of pearls or string of hearts, but make sure these guys get a good light source. Avoid big statement plants like the cheese plant, as this lot will get cramped. Instead, mini-plants will love showing off here.

Step 3. Dress up
When it comes to pots, mix it up. Use different sizes, textures and colours. Old with new. Geometric with wonky! I love putting prickly cacti in a dainty china teacup next to a concrete pot holding a smooth mother-in-law's tongue. Experiment. I discovered terracotta and copper make a wicked pairing when I moved the shelves around in one of our shops.

Step 4. Pose
When it comes to placing your pots, there is nothing more boring than a row of the same things. Again, mix up textures to create impact and don't get me started on odd numbers. Trailing, climbing and bushy plants will also break up the geometric shapes of the shelves. Which shelf to place your plant on will depend on how much light it gets or how much it trails – just keep an eye out and move the ones that look unhappy.

Rating
An easy-going relationship

Name check
The leaves look like hearts. They've even got a lacy pattern on them. Naughty.

The deets
The string of hearts is actually a hanging succulent, which means that it needs very little watering. I like to sell them as an alternative Valentine's Day gift for girls to give to their fellas. They make a striking present and always sell out when I put them on my shelves. Display in a hanging macramé to show off your new beau.

Back to the roots
These guys were discovered hanging from rocks at an altitude of 1,800 feet so they love full sunshine. They also tolerate temperature changes and high humidity making the bathroom a perfect home. Interestingly, this clever succulent will change colour depending on its environment: in low light the leaves turn a lighter shade of green, but in full sun you will find it goes a richer, seaweed green. Enjoy the sculptural, decorative vines by trailing them from a bathroom shelf and marvel at their cascading prowess.

How not to kill your string of hearts
Heartbreak is easily avoided with this easy, easy plant. It is prone to rot, though, so if you see yellow leaves, your baby is too wet. To avoid this sad ending, give it enough drink to drench the soil, but allow the soil to dry out completely before watering again. It goes dormant in winter, so water even less frequently then. These guys are vulnerable to pest attacks so keep a watchful eye.

Plants in art

MATISSE

Matisse is a man after my own heart – he kept things simple! Like an abstract florist he created his work just using a pair of scissors and an open mind. He liked to break free from conventions, too, covering his walls from floor to ceiling with cut-outs made from brightly painted paper, 'I have made a little garden all around me where I can walk,' Matisse noted.

Just looking at one of Matisse's cut-outs will conjure images of the holey monstera leaf. He surrounded himself with cheese plants in his studio at the Hôtel Régina, Nice, and a scroll through Pinterest will bring up pictures of a very handsome one, looking big, bold and very happy, with huge leaves spreading out across the room – enjoying the southern French climate, no doubt. Matisse filled his life with plants and it is a scientific fact that houseplants make you more creative, so… just saying.

FRIDA KAHLO

Frida Kahlo is my personal fave. I have her portrait up in the shop and raise my mono-less brow to her every now and then when I need some inspiration. Fellow Kahlo followers will know her signature style: colours, textures, brow and, of course, plants and flowers. The flowers are said to hold a huge significance, as they were often taken from her private garden in Mexico. Frida's garden was a work of art in itself, filled with native Mexican plants mixed with European varieties. Cacti hung out with rows of geraniums, and inside her house, Kahlo would arrange varying combinations of marigolds, blue and white irises, dahlias, calla lilies and violets. Native plants also appeared as floral crowns in her self-portraits, telling the viewer the story of her own roots. She is said to have remarked that she painted plants and flowers so that they would not die and that the flower appealed to her because its unopened buds resemble a heart. One of her lovers, the Spanish artist Josep Bartolí, recalled Kahlo saying, 'Fruits are like flowers – they speak to us in provocative language and teach us things that are hidden.'

DAVID HOCKNEY

Every morning, Hockney's boyfriend places flowers at the end of his bed (take note, plant dads!). Instead of hiding under the duvet and scrolling through Instagram, Hockney began experimenting with a painting app on his phone and started documenting the morning ritual of flowers from his pillow. Twenty of his closest friends began receiving emails with iPhone-painted flowers attached, 'I draw flowers every day on my iPhone and send them to my friends, so they get fresh flowers every morning'. I might not advocate a quick fix for florals, but I love this idea. In fact, I've just started doing Watercolour Wednesdays in my shop with the illustrator of this book, Bloody Bishop, where people can observe plants through a different lens. iPads not included.

DUTCH MASTERS

The Dutch painters' fascination with flowers can be traced back to the sixteenth century when developments in science saw an interest in botany bloom. By the 1630s, prices for the most coveted bulbs had skyrocketed and the so-called 'tulip mania' began. The Dutch were hooked and, at the turn of the seventeenth century, Dutch painters were among the first artists to produce paintings that exclusively depicted flowers. I'm mad about the Dutch masters but not, I have to say, the earlier paintings. These feature symmetrical arrangements throughout the seasons – very un-G&T! It was over the course of the seventeenth century that trends changed and bouquets became more rock 'n' roll – stiff was out and asymmetrical was in. Mix-matching, mind-blowing, eye-catching displays were immortalised in these paintings, inspiring florists everywhere that rule-breaking runs in the blood. Sadly, by the end of the eighteenth century things started to go straight again, as a more decorative style emerged to reflect 'modern' tastes. Pfft. But we'll always have the good ones to hand whenever we need a little inspiration.

HOW NOT

4

TO KILL YOUR

PLANTS

THE SEVEN DEADLY PLANT SINS

Being a (ahem) good Catholic School Girl, I often need a little prod from on high to get the plant guilt juices flowing. Need some divine intervention? Confess to your plant sins and cross your heart not to do them again.

USING PLANT NAMES IN VAIN
Always, always learn your plant's name. First, it's just good manners. Second, it's essential to know its name to know how to look after it.

FORGETTING THY PLANT
It's not a sin to forget to water your plants once in a while – in fact, many thrive on a little neglect. But the amount of times I see soil so dry it's coming away from the walls of the pot – don't let this happen! Plants need water to live. Nuff said.

SMOTHERING THY PLANT
We are taught to care for all of God's creatures, but over-caring is perhaps the deadliest sin of all – you're literally killing them with kindness. Put the watering can down and wait for the soil to dry out before you water it again.

THE SIN OF ICARUS
And God said, 'Let there be light!'. But not a direct, south-facing sun one in the peak of summer. The glass can refract, adding light intensity that even desert-dwelling cacti won't be used to.

LEADING THEM INTO DARKNESS
Plants need light to live. If you have no light at all, you're gonna have to look at artificial ones. And if you're planning on just replacing your plant every few months, think, 'What would Jesus do?'

BLOWING HOT AND COLD AIR
Vent and be damned! Remove all plants from the path of radiators and air conditioners. Avoid keeping them near front doors, too, where temperatures can flux.

NOT FEEDING THE HUNGRY
A plant uses the nutrients in the soil to stay healthy. When those nutrients run out, you need to stock it back up through feed. Break bread, I mean plant food. Feed once a month.

MAKING YOUR PLANT BABIES BIG, STRONG AND REALLY, REALLY GOOD-LOOKING

When it comes to soil, nutrients and water, things can start to get technical. I have never professed myself to be a scientist, let alone a plant expert – I learn everything on the job. But understanding what a plant needs to live and how to keep it looking HOT is just as important as understanding how not to kill it.

Soil

Not only is soil an anchor for your plant's roots, it provides the water, food and air that your plant baby needs to grow. The right soil should supply your houseplant with the things it would have been able to find naturally back in its own environment – back at its roots! But before you run outside for supplies, put that trowel down. Garden soil will become muddy, dry out like concrete and invite unwanted pests into the home. Luckily, good old potting compost works wonders for most houseplants, as it has sufficient drainage and will store nutrients. However, if you are working with succulents, you'll need something with better drainage to stop those bottoms getting soggy. When it comes to selecting a soil, opt for John Innis – the granddaddy of the good stuff (see more on John Innis, opposite).

A problem for city dwellers is a) lugging massive bags home and b) storing them in a one-bed flat. At Grace & Thorn we'll pot up a bag to suit your size, so see if your local florist will do the same. You'll always need more than you think so ask them to be generous.

Mix it up
Different plants have different needs and some may benefit from a specially selected soil. Regular soil is great for greedy plants, peat (but go for a peat substitute, see below) is an excellent all-rounder, and sand will give the perfect drainage for succulents. Some gardeners mix their own, but luckily John Innis has already done the hard work for us.

The problem with peat
Meet peat, the compost base that is light, cheap and has excellent drainage. Sounds too good to be true, right? Right. Peat is sourced from increasingly rare habitats in the UK and across Europe, killing off the flora and fauna that depend on it. It took Mother Nature around 10,000 years to make these peat bogs, which keep more carbon dioxide out of the atmosphere than forests, but it's taken us only 40 years to almost completely destroy them. Just boycott it and go for a peat substitute instead.

Peat substitute
Peat substitute-based compost is light and stores moisture, so is ideal for rainforest plants who like humid, wet, airy conditions.

It can also be kept constantly damp without becoming soggy, and the texture resembles that of the rainforest floor. Plants with tender roots are also very at home in this compost, as it allows the roots to run free and pick up nutrients compared to sludging through thicker soils. One disadvantage of a peat substitute mix is that it is very light in weight and top-heavy plants may topple over, especially if the mixture dries out.

Potting soil

Soil is rich in plant food so is good for greedy plants who need a regular supply. It releases nutrients to the plant over a long period of time, so leafy palms who like to be undisturbed will be very happy. Also, it is much heavier than peat-based mixtures so will help keep large plants with big leaves from fallling over. However, soil bases can get overly heavy and it is much easier to overwater your plant if it is in soil rather than its more porous cousin, peat or a peat substitute mix.

Sand

Sand or grit is added to mixtures to improve drainage, as the grains are not capable of holding water so they prevent the other material from clumping together. Always use this mix when potting succulents to stop their bottoms getting soggy.

Forgot your coat?

There is nothing smarter than a new coat. The same applies for plants – and they are useful, too. A topcoat layer over the soil stops water from evaporating and prevents bugs from getting in. Use stones, shells or even moss for a fancy look. It's all about personal taste. When coats start to look old, it's time for a new one – refresh or try a new seasonal look.

WHO IS JOHN INNIS ANYWAY?

John Innis is the granddaddy of soils and a Grace & Thorn favourite. However, it is important to note that John Innes is not an actual man who makes compost, but a range of composts developed at the John Innes Institute. John Innes was a property and land dealer in nineteenth-century London who gave his fortune to the improvement of horticulture, and thus the institute came to be. John Innis is a label to look out for when buying compost, mostly because it keeps things nice and simple with options: 1, 2 or 3.

John Innes No. 1

No. 1 has a carefully balanced nutrient content to suit young plants and allow them to grow. Perfect for really little plant babies and propagating cuttings! (See page 215.)

John Innes No. 2

This is the go-to mix for potting up most houseplants and vegetables. No. 2 contains twice the amount of nutrients found in No. 1, so it suits medium-sized plants and will keep them healthy and nourished.

John Innes No. 3

This extra-rich mix is perfect for houseplants who have been on the scene for a while. It's also good for giving home-grown veg a boost.

Feeding time

It took me a while to find my feet when feeding plants. A lot of my plant babies seemed happy and healthy regardless, and, to be frank, it felt like a bit of a faff. But when the nutrients in the soil ran out, I soon saw the need. When you first pot a houseplant, it will have a few months of food stored in its soil, but as they grow up, plants are constantly using up the nutrients and eventually it runs out. Feeding will give them a healthy dose of what does them good. You don't need to do it often, but do keep it consistent – forgetting and giving them a massive meal will just leave them bloated and unhappy. Like with over watering, it's not true that the more you feed your plants the healthier they will be, so only give them what they need. Not sure how much to give your plant? Do your homework. And, as a general rule, when plants are resting in the winter you can undo the apron strings.

Yes, baby!

At Grace & Thorn we love Baby Bio. It's classic, inexpensive and won't take up much space on your shelf. Nonnas all over the world have been using it for the last 60 years. Tried and tested. You can use it every time you water, but we like to use half a capful every couple of weeks to keep things consistent. As with all plant parenting, your babies will have different needs, so remember one cap doesn't necessarily fit all.

Grooming

Haircuts

When someone points out a brown leaf, I point at one of my split ends. What would you do? Cut it off! Always remove dead or broken leaves and stems – it stops the plant putting its energy into old leaves and allows it to concentrate on new growth. Cut as close to the stem as possible but never right against it. If you're pruning for growth, step back and look at its shape and imagine what you want it to be. Don't get too over excited and try not to cut off more than a quarter of your plant – unless you're pruning it back for the winter. The more you cut, the bigger and bushier it will grow back.

(Psst! You can repot healthy plant cuttings from pruning to grow more plant babies! Skip to page 215 to learn how.)

Cleaning

It's important to keep leaves clean. First, so they can carry out their important job of photosynthesis and second, because it makes them look good. Dust can be found hanging out in most houses so when you see it on your plant, get the dust buster out – aka a damp cloth. A little warm water should be fine, but if they need a good scrub, try a one-third soap-to-water mix. Support the leaf in one hand and gently wipe down with the other. For succulents and hairy leaves, use a toothbrush.

Polishing

Polished leaves are your fast track to a super-slick plant baby and there are lots of different methods. My nonna liked to use milk on her fig. Olive oil is another inexpensive shiner – just watch out for dust as it can be a bit sticky. Leave young leaves alone and make sure you are really gentle – don't press down too hard.

Rating
Everyone knows an ant can't move a rubber tree plant, but you can certainly look after it.

Name check
Remember the big rubber leaves which are actually used in the production of rubber.

The deets
Meet the Steady Eddie of plants. This guy is seriously low hassle and just right if you are looking for a statement piece, as they can grow up to 15m! Make sure you've enough space to let it whoosh! It has big, dark, glossy leaves that you need to keep clean by wiping them with a damp sponge.

Back to the roots
The rubber tree comes from hot, moist regions, so it'll appreciate a spritz of water on its leaves occasionally. It likes a drink so water well about once a week or enough to ensure it is kept moist. Indirect light is its favourite but it can get away with low light, and will let you know if it's not getting enough by becoming lanky. These guys grow pretty big. When its pot is too small, you have two choices: 1) repot and keep going, 2) leave it in the same pot but replace the top 10cm of soil to keep it looking fresh.

How not to kill your rubber plant
The leaves are the indicator of whether your rubber plant is happy or not. If they have gone yellow, it could be a sign of over watering or not enough light, so adjust the drink and provide a sunnier home. If the leaves start to droop, it could be too hot or over watered. It's pretty resilient to bugs, but if they appear – fight back! Don't panic if there are raised white dots on the leaves, these are totally normal.

THE AGONY PLANT'S GUIDE TO WATERING

Watering is a big issue. When to, how much, what kind? Watering cans down, people! First, no one size fits all. Every plant has its own needs. Get to know how much your plant baby likes to drink. Watch it and learn — it will soon tell you when it is thirsty. All too much? Then follow these rules:

How much water does my plant like?

Go back to the roots. All plants will order something different at the bar, so the first question to ask is, 'Have you got any I.D.?' Ahem, no, the first question to ask is 'Where does your plant come from?' Plants adapted to a bog life enjoy soaking wet conditions, whereas the succulent family has adapted to long periods of dry between heavy watering. Go back to pages 46–82 to understand how much water your plant needs.

How often should I water?

The finger test: forget fancy tools and calendars, use my foolproof method and stick your finger in it. Well, just the soil, but not just on the top, get it in about 5cm. If the soil is dry, water it. If the soil is damp, leave it alone. If only all things were that simple.

How much should I water at a time?

You've had enough, mate! When the soil is dry, water your plant thoroughly — you want to make sure the roots at the bottom of the pot have had a good drink. Get the spout of your watering can as close to the base of the plant as possible. If your container has holes, keep watering until you see water coming out into the saucer. Wait a few minutes and then empty the saucer so the plant doesn't sit around with a soggy bottom. If your pot doesn't have holes, you're going to need to watch the watering as the same soggy bottom warning applies. Keep going until the soil starts to flood — the trick is to let it thoroughly dry out before you water again. You'll soon know if you're overdoing it, as your plant won't be happy. Be careful about getting the leaves wet too, as lots of plants don't like it.

What kind of water should I give my plant? Still or sparkling?

There is a lot of fuss about what different types of water to give your plant (rain, bottled etc.). But who is honestly going to collect rainwater? In most situations, good old tap water won't cause any problems. But if you live in a 'soft water' area you might need to be a little cautious. This is because soft water contains lots of salts, which build up in the

soil and stop the natural transfer of minerals and water into the roots. To avoid this happening, 'flush' the pot once every couple of months. This just involves pouring in bottled water to wash the salt build-up out of the drainage holes.

When should I water my plant?
Rise and shine! It is best to water plants in the morning because it gives them a chance to dry out during the day. Watering at night leaves plants damp making it easier for the fungal Bogie Man to come out. Water more in the summer too, when they are actively growing and less in the winter when they are resting.

GOOD LUCK AND KEEP IT GREEN.

The Agony Plant
xoxo

BATH TIME ~

I'm all about saving time and getting a job done quickly (but
efficiently). Every now and then, I will get all the plants from
upstairs and place them in the bath and give them a lovely warm
shower! Don't go too mental and drown them, just give them a
good drink (no desert plants here, please). And make sure none
of your sick plants go in with the healthy ones as they may spread
their germs!

WHAT'S WRONG WITH
MY PLANT?

No plant in my house looks like it did when I bought it. Everything is bigger, bushier and bashed by whippets. Don't be a fusspot; your plant baby is growing, let it be free! All good plant parents should step back and observe how their plants grow to learn what makes them happy and sad. This way you can spot problems as they arise. The amount of people who come into my shop sobbing over a brown leaf. I just get a pair of scissors and snip it off! It's when the leaves suddenly look eaten or dry, or the stalks are thin or wilting that you need to take note. But don't panic just yet, often these things are easy fixes such as watering or re-positioning.

When it comes to pests, they are part and parcel of houseplant life. As long as you have plants, insects will want to eat them! You need to act quickly though, so your other plants don't get infected. Put the poorly plant in quarantine until it's better. As always, different plants have different issues so always go back to their roots, but take action if you spot the following signs.

Leaves turn yellow

Don't panic, it's normal for lower leaves on an older plant to turn yellow and fall off. When lots of leaves across the whole plant do this though, watch the watering! Over watering is a common cause of poorly looking leaves. Let the roots dry out before watering again. If the roots are soaking, check it into the houseplant hospital (see page 208) to dry out.

Ends of leaves turn brown

Again, this is a common watering problem. You're either over or under watering, so watch the drink. Another cause could be that your plant baby is too hot! Is it near a south-facing window or a radiator? Lower the heat and see how it gets on. Your plant might also not be getting enough humidity so get misting.

Leaves fall off

Remember, one or two that fall off is normal, but any more is a sign you could be over watering. Let the soil dry out and cut back on the drink. Also, is your plant near a draught? Move it where the temperature is more even.

Leaves get spots

Your poor guy is getting sunburnt! Filter out direct rays or move it somewhere else. This could also be a case of bacterial leaf spot. Wet and dark conditions promote the formation of these bacteria so try improving the light conditions and reduce the humidity. Pick off affected leaves to stop it spreading.

Limp leaves

You're over or under watering. Watch the drink and check your guy isn't too hot. If that fails, maybe it's time for a repot?

Leaves rolling up

What could be happening is that your plant is conserving energy by reducing its surface area. As long as the leaves roll back out, this is just a clever characteristic of your plant! If they don't roll flat, watch the watering.

Crispy edges

The most common cause is over watering. Plants pass water from their roots to their leaves, but when a plant has had too much to drink, the excess water builds at the leaf edge until they burst and turn crispy. Time to check in to the houseplant hospital to dry out.

Leaves chewed

Aha, now is the time to call pest control. Check out the teeth marks to discover the perpetrator and check the plant in to your houseplant hospital to sort the symptoms. Quarantine the poorly plant to stop your other plants falling to the same chewed fate.

Mould on the soil

Don't worry, just take it off! Change the topcoat for a fresh look (see page 197).

Slow growth

Plants need light to grow and your plant isn't getting enough. Move it somewhere sunnier. Also make sure it's getting all the nutrients it needs, so check its dietary requirements.

Wobbly bits

When it comes to removing dead, broken, bitten or scorched leaves, think of it like having a broken nail – what would you do? We've all accidentally broken a stem so don't try and hide it, as they are susceptible to disease. And no, it's not going to stick itself back together with magic plant glue. Just get rid. It's good practice to cut troubled leaves and branches off to allow the plant to put its energy into the good stuff. Give them a good snip near the base with a pair of sharp scissors and make sure the wound is clean.

HOUSEPLANT HOSPITAL

Nursing your plant babies back to health is a rewarding part of being a plant parent. If your plants are really sick, you will need a space for a houseplant hospital – somewhere poorly patients can stay until they are better and can go home to the plant family. Find somewhere light but shaded, so your plants can get a little life into their leaves without getting scorched. Keep things clean: make sure your houseplant hospital is free from pollutants. Did you know ferns hate smoking? Fags outside, please. But if your plant isn't likely to affect the rest of the gang, then they can probably stay where they are. Here are the most common ailments you'll be treating.

YOUR PLANT IS IN THE WRONG PLACE

OK, in this instance you will definitely need to move your plant! Location can be a major cause of an unhappy plant. Follow our back to the roots guide to find your plant baby's perfect home (see pages 46–82). Don't be nervous about moving plants around – a change is as good as a holiday, remember. Although sometimes it can be as simple as rotating your plant in the position it is already in. Often, light won't be reaching round to the back and your plant will start to go wonky. Get into the habit of regularly turning your pots so they get an even distribution of light on all the leaves.

YOUR PLANT IS AT THE WRONG TEMPERATURE: THE GOLDILOCKS TEST

Some houseplants can be a bit fussy. Here's how to spot if your plants are too hot, too cold or just right.

Too hot!
Symptoms: Blooms don't last long, lanky growth or lower leaf problems, such as wilting.
Treatment: Make sure your plant is away from radiators and not blasted by direct sunlight.

Too cold!
Symptoms: Leaves curl up and the curled leaves can turn brown and fall off.
Treatment: Is your plant near a doorway or draught? Move it somewhere where the temperature is more constant.

Just right
You've got a good-looking, happy plant. Goldilocks would be proud.

YOUR PLANT IS OVER OR UNDER WATERED

Rehab
We've all done it: either got a bit over excited with the watering can or ignored our plant babies when work's been busy. Listen up! If you do it regularly, your poor plant is going

to get poorly. BUT you may be able to rectify things with these tricks.

Under watering
Symptoms: Dropping stems and leaves are a huge sign your plant is thirsty. Leaf edges may become brown and the lower leaves may curl and turn yellow. In the worst cases, the soil will pull away from the sides – but if that's happening, you really need to take better care of your baby.
Treatment: Remove your plant from direct sunlight. Place your plant in a bowl of water (in the bath, preferably) and leave to soak for 30 minutes. Pull out the plug and let the plant drain for another 10 minutes, and then put it back into the pot. Fingers crossed.

Over watering
Symptoms: If you are over watering, you'll notice a general squelch going on: flowers become mouldy, leaves get brown patches and roots turn mushy. A really noticeable sign is young and old leaves falling off together.
Treatment: First, remove your plant from direct sunlight – keep your cool, both of you. Remove the plant from the pot and wrap it in kitchen towel or newspaper until the excess water has been absorbed. Repot and let it dry out completely before you water again.

DOES MY PLANT HAVE ROOT ROT?

What is root rot?
This is when part of the root rots (obvs), but this isn't something to make light of. Root rot is a serious issue that means it might be time to start planning a plant funeral. It occurs when plants have been well and truly over watered. The excess water makes it very difficult for the roots to get the air that they need, causing them to decay. Another cause can be fungus

in the soil. The fungus can lay dormant in the soil and then suddenly raise its ugly head when the plant is overwatered.
Symptoms: If the plant is showing signs mentioned above for seemingly unknown reasons, you will want to check the roots. Get out your newspaper, remove the plant from the pot and loosen the soil to observe the roots. The roots affected by root rot will look black and will feel mushy. Affected roots may literally fall off the plant when you touch them. Make sure you don't confuse rotting roots with healthy roots that are naturally black or pale – always give them a squeeze: if they're firm they're fine.
Treatment: Whether the problem is over watering or a fungus flare-up, you must act quickly. Check your infected plant into your houseplant hospital ASAP to give it the best chance of survival. Plants with prolonged root rot should be given up for dead, but all is not lost! Usually you can propagate the plant to start life again (see page 215).

DOES MY PLANT NEED ROOT ROT SURGERY?

Brown and mushy roots: I'm afraid there is nothing we can do.
Firm and white roots: Trim back the roots and cut away any leaves or stems showing rot. Repot after two days.
Damp and sad-looking roots: A clear case of root rot. Follow the procedure below.

Treating root rot
Use your fingers to remove the big clumps of soil from the roots, then hold the roots under running water to gently wash away any remaining soil. Next, use a clean pair of sharp scissors to trim away all of the remaining affected roots – you may have to

remove a big chunk of the root system if the plant is badly affected. If you want to make extra sure that fungus isn't the problem, dip the remaining roots in a fungicide solution. Now, clean your scissors with alcohol and cut back about one-third of the plant itself. This will help it get better more quickly, by having fewer leaves to put its energy into. Wash the offending pot thoroughly and repot the plant in fresh potting mix. Keep it in a bright spot without direct sunlight and don't water again until new roots appear. While the plant is growing its new roots, do not give it any food as this may stress it out. Keep an eye on the patient and when it is happy and healthy, it can rejoin the plant family.

YOUR PLANT DOESN'T HAVE ENOUGH HUMIDITY

Humidity is rising...
Symptoms: If your plant is from a lovely warm, moist, tropical clime and you put it somewhere where the air is cold and dry, it ain't gonna be happy. Watch the leaves – are they browning, shrivelling, wilting and dropping off? These are all signs that your humidity level is low. Time to turn up the humidity. Try a treatment below.

Pebble tray
Put about a 2.5cm layer of pebbles into a tray and fill halfway with water. Now set your pots on top. The water underneath will raise the humidity around your plants. Never let the water cover the top of the pebbles and rinse out every so often.

Misting
Misting is the simplest way to up the humidity. Simply spray evenly over the whole plant. Remember that not all plants like to be misted,

so always go back to the roots of your plant to see what they need (see pages 46–82).

Grouping
Plants release moisture through their leaves in a process called transpiration, so grouping them together increases the humidity around them all.

Double potting
You can pot your little pot inside a larger one with soil that you keep constantly damp. The moisture evaporating from the damp soil will raise the humidity.

YOUR PLANT HAS A PEST INFECTION

Scale insects
Symptoms: Brown, small, shelled insects love houseplants. You'll find these tiny guys sucking on stems and leaves, which might feel sticky or sooty to touch. Also, check underneath the leaf to see if there are white eggs.
Treatment: Remember to put your infected plant in quarantine as soon as possible. Once it's there, scrub off the scale using an old toothbrush. If they won't budge, get that bottle of cheap vodka someone left from a party down from the shelf and rub the leaves with it. Sober up the plant with fresh water. Keep an eye on the patient with regular washing to make sure the infestation has gone and send it home when ready.

Mealy bugs
Symptoms: White, oval insects that, en masse, look like cotton wool. These guys

thrive in warm conditions, hence their love for houseplants. You'll notice a fluffy white texture on top of the leaves and a black mass forming on the leaf itself. Check underneath for pinky-coloured eggs, too.
Treatment: Remove the patient as soon as possible and place it in quarantine. Treat by mixing a tablespoon of liquid soap with a litre of water and spritz the buggers off! Give the plant a rinse and remove any infested or dead leaves, as they may still have bugs in them. Keep the patient in quarantine for a month to make sure the pests have gone.

Aphids
Symptoms: Tiny and green with typical insect-like bodies, you will usually find them hanging out in packs.
At first glance it may look like there is a strange texture covering your plant until you look more closely and realise it's these blighters!
Treatment: Luckily, these guys can be washed off in the shower. Put your plant in and give them a blast. Make sure you protect your plant's roots by covering the pot with a plastic bag. If they won't budge, get the garlic breath on them! Mix a few cloves of garlic into your mister and give them a massive honk. As always, keep the plant in quarantine until you are sure the pests are gone.

Red spider mites
Symptoms: Red insects so small you'll need a magnifying glass. But don't be fooled, these guys may be tiny but they are troublesome.
Infected plants will have a dusty-looking surface on the bottom side of their leaves, but look closer and you might see the dust is moving! If so, you've got mites, mate. If you see faint webs, your plant is pretty infested.
Treatment: Mite mums can have a hundred babies, so it's really easy for your other plants to get sick. Move infected plants immediately and keep them apart from the rest of your plant family. Wash the leaves well with soap spray (see mealy bugs on page 210) and give the patient a good scrub in the bath.

Fungus gnats
Symptoms: Fungus gnats, or the Bogey Men to you and me, are small flies that infest potting mix with their maggot-looking babies! Watch out for groups of flies hovering around the soil or a near the window. These pests don't affect humans but when their gnat babies get into the soil, your plant baby's roots need help!
Treatment: Let the roots dry out completely and remove any poor-looking soil. This will kill off the larvae and put off gnat mums from laying their baby gnats there. Yellow fly-catching tape will also help.

CHEMICAL BROTHER

A big question for any plant parent when your plant gets infected is do you want to use chemicals or not? There are endless chemicals in the garden centre, but most pesticides are actually based on plain old soap and water. At Grace & Thorn, we like to give nature a helping hand whenever we can and so we try to keep things natural. There is nothing wrong with sticking it under the shower and blasting them off with water, *Ghostbusters*-style! Or just use an empty cleaning spray – just rinse the bottle thoroughly before you use it.

THE AGONY PLANT'S GUIDE TO GOING ON HOLIDAY

Leaving your plant babies home alone can be nerve-racking. If it's just a weekend away, relax, they'll cope fine — but anything longer (you lucky thing) will require a little more preparation. Succulents and cacti are the grown-ups of the family, so let them do their own thing. Ferns, on the other hand, are a little trickier. If in doubt, maybe call a plant babysitter (i.e. your friendly neighbour).

Summer hols or Christmas break
It's important to remember that plants have different needs in summer and winter. If you're off on your summer hols, think about what you're looking forward to — lots of drink, a bit of sunshine, no sunburn — your plant is probably feeling the same. Give your plants an extra big drink before you head off. Don't worry about drowning them, they'll just take the nutrients they need. Make sure they've dried out before watering again. Consider moving plants to a cooler room or somewhere with more shade to stop them drying out.

In winter, some plants will be in hibernation, getting ready for spring. When you are cosying up on chilly nights, a few of your plants might like to be cosy, too, while others — like cacti — would rather stay cold. We all know how hard it can be in the party season but most houseplants need to lay off the drink in winter. Water lightly before you go, so the compost is moist but not soaked. Windows can get extra cold in winter, so move plants away to keep them warm.

Holiday pedi
You've done your holiday beauty prep so make sure your plants are looking their best, too. Remove dead petals or leaves and give the surface of the soil a little rake to keep it looking fresh.

The shoelace trick
If you're feeling crafty, get a shoelace (twine will also do) and put one end into the soil and another into a vase filled with water. The shoelace sucks the water from the vase into the soil.

Keep it consistent
Try to make sure the temperature won't drop below what they've been used to. It may feel a bit extravagant but if you can afford to time your heaters, give your plants a bit of love while you're away. Better yet, get a plant babysitter who could do with staying cosy.

DON'T FORGET TO SEND A POSTCARD.

The Agony Plant
xoxo

How to hold a plant funeral

So now we've all admitted to killing plants, how do we give them the send-off they deserve? There is nothing sadder than seeing a dead plant left on display. It's time to say goodbye. Here is the Grace & Thorn guide to dealing with plant grief.

Stage 1. Admit closure
The first question is, is it actually dead? A lot of plants can look pretty unhappy, but with a bit of TLC will come back to life (see pages 208–212). Check the roots and stem of the plant – if they are mushy, or break in your hands, it's time to admit defeat. If it's winter, question whether your plant is just having a bit of time off! Like a lot of things in nature, some plants will hibernate in the winter to store energy for flowering again in the spring. Go back to the roots and check its habits before letting it hit the dust.

Stage 2. Chuck
If it's definitely dead. Time to chuck it. Check your local recycling rules for the plant itself

and why not scatter the soil in your local park to help new life grow?

Stage 3. Mourn
The best way to deal with a plant death is to face up to the facts. Why did it die? What made it unhappy? By learning through your mistakes, you can make sure your new plant babies won't suffer the same fate.

Stage 4. Look forward
You now have a space for a new member of your plant family! If a snazzy pot has become available, make sure to wash it before giving it a new companion. Check the ratings on our favourite plants in this book and maybe go for something a little less needy.

How to bring your plants back to life

Propagating is your excuse to play Plant God – you take one plant and you turn it into many (or is that Plant Jesus?). It saves money, it is easy to do and it makes a great present. And if those weren't enough good reasons, plants want you to do it. Sound heavenly? Read on.

Steps to plant heaven
- Propagate during spring and summer for optimum growth
- Always try a few cuttings to increase chances of success
- Invest in some 'rooting formula' to help baby stems grow
- Give your cuttings more attention; these guys need help to get going

Stem cuttings
Taking stem cuttings is the easiest method, as you can take several snips to increase your chances of success. Cut healthy-looking stems when they are about 12cm – but not when they're flowering. Use a very sharp knife to cut below the leaf joint. Remove any lower leaves, then dip the stem into your 'rooting formula'. Take a pot with soil and make a hole with a pencil, insert your cutting and firm it in.

Leaf cuttings
For plants that do not have stems (a nod to succulents here), try leaf cuttings instead. Cut the leaf as near to the base as possible. For big juicy succulents, let the leaf dry out for a couple of days. When it is dry, push the cut end of the leaf into your soil at a 45-degree angle, taking care to not get soil on the actual leaf. Increase the humidity (see page 210) around the cutting and wait for new growth.

Plantlets
The spider plant swan song. When it is dying, it will send out babies (plantlets) to grow again. When the plantlets have developed roots, snip off, pot up and water well. Within a few weeks you should notice new growth.

Offsets
Some houseplants produce miniature plants to the side of the mainstem. When the offset is about half the size of the parent plant, cut it off as close to the mainstem as possible. The trick is to preserve as much of the baby's roots as possible, otherwise it won't survive. Pot the parent and baby in separate pots, keeping the baby in a pot just bigger than its roots.

Division
Sometimes it's just a simple matter of splitting up fuller plants. Remove the plant from its pot and gently divide it up, pulling the roots apart with your hands. If the roots are tough, use a clean sharp knife to separate or slice them apart. Repot the new sections into individual pots that are a little bigger than their roots.

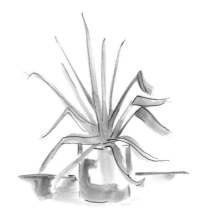

NIK'S
FIDDLE
FABLE

As a child growing up on a London estate, the fiddle leaf fig tree growing in the front room of my grandparents' house had me mesmerised. My nonna would tell me stories about this fiddle leaf fig, drawing on her own Italian childhood in Puglia, so far removed from mine, it was if she had plucked it from a fairytale. Regaling one of her memories, she described the tree as her favourite hiding spot during games of hide and seek with her sister. After telling one of these tales of the tree, she would disappear and I would hear the fridge door open, followed by the clink of old-fashioned milk bottles. With this sound I knew it was feeding time – for the fiddle leaf fig, that is. A jug of milk would be handed to me, along with an old rag and a stool to climb on. I would play the story back in my head, a happy tree that grows and grows, loved and fed once a week through its leaves. I'd soak the cloth in the milk, ring it out and then carefully wipe each leaf with the magic elixir. I would tend to every leaf believing the old wives' tale that the milk fed the leaves and made the plant strong. I have since looked into it and have discovered that milk is great purely for making the leaves shiny. Grazie, nonna!

I believe it was the amazing fact that the tree existed within the walls of a house(!), not in a park, that made this a specimen of awe and wonder for a city child. When I opened Grace & Thorn, these were, without doubt, going to be my first babies, a chance to offer plant fantasy within urban dwellings, no longer exclusive to off-the-wall Crouch End grandparents.

Rating
Like all A-listers, this one needs attention.

Name check
Fiddle-shaped leaves. Tree-shaped posture. The fig leaf part? Think of the leaf dancing a 'jig' to the fiddle. Olé!

The deets
With its big floppy leaves, the fiddle leaf fig is the tease of the plant world. You'll fall madly in love, but it'll keep you on your toes. And you won't be the first to fall for its charm. It is the structural shape of the tree that gives it its appeal – a tall thin trunk supports large bowing leaves. The leathery texture of the leaves is also captivating in the home, waving cheekily to anyone who gives it a glance. And it looks really good in a picture. Like really good. This is your statement piece to show off, but mark my word, you'll be working hard behind the scenes.

Fact!
What might explain its louche behaviour is that the Ficus has already given its heart away, to the wasp. Each member of the Ficus family requires one specific wasp in order to pollinate and blossom. The wasp will only lay eggs within its matched Ficus.

Back to the roots
The fiddle leaf fig grows on the floor of the tropical rainforest, so indirect light is your sweet spot. Too much and the leaves will burn; too little and they'll shrivel. The best thing is to experiment with the right spot, but lugging it around may require an extra pair of hands. A lot of people tell you not to move your fiddle fig as it will go into shock, but I am yet to meet one who doesn't like a bit of sightseeing. Only water when the soil becomes slightly dry and always let the soil dry out before you water again. The worst thing to do is to over water or water too little in the winter. Those tropical temperatures are pretty warm, so constant house heat will suit it fine, just keep it well away from cold draughts. To keep that lovely tree-like shape, prune the plant when it is still fairly young to encourage big bushy growth. With all the showing off, you're going to want a nice-looking pot to dress your plant up. It looks great in white, but if you find this a bit overdone, why not consider a wicker coat? Just make sure you don't go too big on the pot size – despite all its flirting, it will get stage fright.

How not to kill your fiddle leaf fig
First, it's quite normal for the bottom leaves to drop off when it's growing – they are making space for the new ones. When more leaves start to fall though, you need to check light, watering and air. If the leaves lose their colour or become brown at the edges, it's thirsty. If the leaves become soft or develop brown patches, hold off the drink. Don't panic! Even after an ill patch your plant baby can still be Instagrammable. Remove any leaves that have had it and just trim off the brown parts of the leaves that are OK.

FIDDLE LEAF FIG *Ficus lyrata*

FREE YOUR

5

FLOWERS

BOLD BOUQUETS

When I opened Grace & Thorn, I was tired of seeing tight bouquets struggling to breathe, so I decided to do my own thing and encourage flowers to dance and sing! Flowers are my creative output. It's like having paint and a brush in front of me. When it comes to flower arranging, I encourage you all to break the rules. They'll tell you to keep it straight – go wonky. I love asymmetry, clashing colours, pastels with a dark pinch of colour. It's not just about creating a nice bouquet; you need that edge to draw your eye in, something that makes the bouquet stand out. In fact, it's how I decided on the name Grace & Thorn. I was inspired by the beauty and gracefulness of the rose, but it has a darker side, too: a thorn that says, 'Don't f*&k with me!'. This philosophy runs through my arrangements. They look beautiful, but they sometimes have an almost ballsy attitude. I am sure many florists would tut-tut at my teaching methods, but I think it is important to allow creative freedom to show off the flowers in their purest form and full glory.

The first evidence of a flower arrangement comes from Egypt more than four-and-a-half thousand years ago! Carvings found in tombs show the sacred lotus flower displayed in bowls, vases and arranged with berries. In ancient China, flowers became a ritual offering among Buddhists. Monks brought their knowledge to Japan where the first and oldest school of floral art, the Ikenobō, was founded in the fifteenth century.

In the seventeenth century intrepid explorers introduced new plants and flowers to Europe – where our favourite Dutch painters began documenting these new displays (see page 190). This led to no respectable aristocratic home being without a bunch, and tulip fever in Amsterdam meant the bloom became more valuable than gold! Louis XIV's Versailles palace upped the style and size ante (the French always do), but as social life moved from palaces to Paris, displays soon became more intimate. The nature-lovin' Victorians created a 'language of flowers', sending hidden messages within the flower choices they used. Roses meant love, peonies meant bashfulness, and so on. In big houses (Downton-style), displays were done by the housekeeper, but the art of flower arranging was soon considered a skill 'all young ladies should acquire' – the most popular style being a single display in a small vase. Chic!

By the turn of the twentieth century, every respectable flower lover was reading *Flower Decoration in the House* by Gertrude Jekyll, who affirmed the bouquet's impact on good interior design. As the rules of floristry began to be written by countless women's magazines, publications and a TV presenter or two, floristry pioneers like Constance Spry tried to break them, but things still stayed pretty symmetrical. Rules, rules and more rules. Floristry needs a kick up the bunch. It's time to shake off traditions and free your flowers, Grace & Thorn-style.

Free your flowers

> 'People from a planet without flowers would
> think we must be mad with joy the whole time
> to have such things about us.'
> *Dame Iris Murdoch*

Let flowers dance and sing
Put flowers together as they are in nature,
where everything sits happily alongside
each other without fighting for space. Let the
flowers breathe (they actually last longer that
way) – let them have a good old rave up!

Don't follow the trends
I don't like the idea of nature fallng in and out
of fashion. Instead, I like to let nature make
the rules and then I feast on the goodies that
are in season. I always encourage brides to
think seasonally, too. If you've got your heart
set on one flower but it's the wrong time of
year, you'll be able to find a seasonal one
that is just as beautiful.

Break the rules
Formal training in flower arranging tends to
focus on the idea of creating a perfect dome,
so that your bouquet of flowers can stand
up on its own. My bouquets never stood
up. I love asymmetry. I'd get told off all the
time, but it made my work stand out. I've not
exactly banned the word 'dome' in my shop,
but do I like to go a bit wild instead.

Be wonky
It's all about the angling for me so I never put
flowers straight upright into the vase. I like to
think of it like a clock, saying to myself as I put
them in at these angles: '1 o'clock, 4 o'clock,
9 o'clock. Rock.'

Bring the outside in
I love walking around my neighbourhood
and seeing what's in bloom. I live next to
Epping Forest, where there is an abundance
of nature. Autumn is my favourite time of year,
as the hedgerows become full of berries.
I love to pick bunches and take them home
to fill my house.

Play with colour
I love being able to play with colour. Keep
it green, blue, pink! Clashing colours are a
great way to create impact. I have a bit of a
dislike for the colour white being used with
anything other than more white or green.
On occasion you can pull it off, if it's used
with softer colours, but I have seen it being
used with maroons, oranges and reds and
it's not my bag.

Go wild
Just when you think you've gone wild.
Go 100 per cent wilder.

Seasonal trends

Like fashion, flowers change from season to season and when the weather changes I'm always excitedly looking out of the window hoping to see nature's latest collection. Once upon a time, a train from Cornwall would head through the night delivering fresh flowers to London. This marked the start of spring in the flower trade, bringing bluebells and primroses picked fresh from nature's display. The globalisation of the flower trade means you can now get flowers out of season at all times of the year. But for me, bringing the outside in, rather than forcing it, is what Mother Nature intended. When I do weddings, a lot of brides want flowers that are out of season and I always show them that there are seasonal alternatives. For example, a recent wedding called for big bunches of mimosa but it was the wrong time of year. Instead we used forsythia, which was in season and looked just as stunning. Spring is abundant for flowers and although you might see winter as sparse, this is the time to let foliage shine with holly and berries all fresh from the hedgerows.

SPRING

The warmer weather and longer days slowly wake up nature's most delicate and delightful blooms. When the clocks bounce forward, we get a hint of what's to come with bursts of colour and trees groaning with blossom. Try adding large stems of blossom to vases around the house – simple but very impactful.
G&T faves: *apple blossom, forsythia, nigella, fritillaria, ammi, daffodils*

SUMMER

See ya later morning frost, summer is here! Flowers and foliage are in full bloom with the sun bringing out the big show-offs. The air is filled with scents from so many flowers, from lavender to sweet peas. Heaven!
G&T faves: *waxflower, achillea, foxglove, spirea, cosmos, peony*

AUTUMN

Autumn is my favourite time of year: it's when it all comes in. So many textures! Nature is in abundance! So go forage! There's nothing more satisfying than filling up an array of mixed-sized jars with berries and foliage from the garden.
G&T faves: *dahlia, poppy, mimosa, mottled hydrangea, scabiosa, ranunculus*

WINTER

It may be getting gloomy but nature is still in bloom, full of seasonal flowers to bring colour into your home and the hedgerows are bursting with foliage. Winter is the best for berries and thistles galore, so get those involved, too. Don't overlook the smaller blooms either.
G&T faves: *anemones, hellebores, asclepias, lilac, viburnum, amaryllis*

Our favourite flowers

ENGLISH ROSE

The deets
It's very hard to pick a favourite flower, but the rose has always been important to me. My nan had roses everywhere and their scent always reminds me of her house. I've always loved rosewater products for their smell – did you know it's really easy to make? Just boil the petals and then strain the water into a fancy bottle.

Back to the roots
There are more than one hundred species of rose from all over the world and rose fossils can be traced back 35 million years, found inside Egyptian tombs. It seems like everyone loves the smell of the rose and they were used for their scent long before they were cultivated for the home and garden. Roses started appearing in art about 5,000 years ago. One of my favourite rose paintings is The Meditative Rose by Salvador Dali.

Green skills
Traditionally, roses are used for weddings and funerals, but at G&T, we like to use them in bouquets to create unusual symmetry with smaller flowers. Roses don't have to be kept to Valentine's Day either; go for a string of hearts houseplant instead and enjoy roses all year long.

DAHLIAS

The deets
This beautiful bloom is a Grace & Thorn favourite. Its stunning colours range from vibrant, vivid and sometimes almost neon to variegated and muted. It blossoms from midsummer through to the first frost of autumn and produces many flowers along the way. They are your statement BIG BOLD BLOOM. The bigger the bloom, the greater the impact. They pack a massive punch. With thousands of different varieties, dahlias come in all different shapes, from the pom pom to the spiky and everything in between.

Back to the roots
The first dahlias originated from the hills and mountains of Mexico. They were discovered by the botanical explorer Alexander von Humboldt, who sent the seeds to be cultivated at the botanical gardens of Madrid. The original French diva, Marie Antoinette, fell head over heels for dahlias when they were a new arrival in Europe, and a variety was named after her. In Geneva, J. Wallner cultivated the dahlia for over 40 years, amassing a personal collection of almost 3,000 varieties! This special new-world flower soon caught the imagination of Britain with over 1,400 cultivars blossoming across the country. Summer borders, patios and vases curtsied gracefully to this versatile bloom.

Green skills
Arrange dahlias with mixed wild foliage, creating large exaggerated gestures for impact. Play with three different colours and styles, combining rounded types with spiky varieties for depth. If you are using the brighter-coloured dahlias, temper them with rich, deep blooms and another colour variant.

ANEMONES

The deets
In the language of flowers, anemone means 'daughter of the wind', and they are also known as 'the windflower', because the wind blows the petals open... whoosh! It is said that the plant was created by the goddess Venus when she sprinkled nectar on the blood of her dead lover, Adonis. Romantic by nature, they flower between October and May – perfect for winter and spring weddings. Their natural foliage acts as a kind of skirt, surrounding and framing the petals, helping the flower stand out. We especially love them for their colours though, which are the most incredible autumnal and winter hues – from super-dark centres to petals ranging from rich burgundies and blues to pale pinks.

Back to the roots
These guys are part of the Ranunculaceae family, which hail from sunny climates. There are about 150 different species that grow as wildflowers in Europe, in North America and in Japan. Confusingly, the famous Japanese anemone is not really from Japan, but was developed by botanists in Europe. This species is particularly popular because it is so easy to grow and, quite frankly, looks so pretty.

Green skills
Take advantage of how delicate and papery-looking they are to create contrast. Pair with strong partners, like roses, or hairy foliage, like asparagus fern, so they stand their ground. They look amazing as a statement flower, off-centre in your bouquet. Handle with care so you don't damage the petals.

HYDRANGEAS

The deets
One of my absolute faves! I keep dried hydrangeas in my kitchen (tip: dry them on a radiator) and love using them in displays. These flowers are all about their amazing colour, which is almost indescribable. The colour of the flower actually depends on the pH levels in the soil in which they grow, and they range from blues (acidic) to pinks (alkaline) and everything in between. My friend told me that hydrangeas are going missing from gardens in France because teenagers like to smoke dried petals to get high! But for most of us, it is their beauty that intoxicates us. Tricky houseplants though. I tend to use the cut variety to bring them into my home, but if you're insistent, keep the plants cool and don't let them dry out.

Back to the roots
Native to Asia and the Americas, the biggest clue to understanding the hydrangea is in the name, which originates from the Greek *hydro*, meaning water, and *angeion*, meaning vessel. So these guys love a drink! If yours start to look tired, float them in a sink filled with cold water for 3–4 hours and they'll soon freshen up. Hydrangeas are happiest when they are by the sea (who isn't?) because of the extra moisture in the air. They flower from late spring to late autumn, but drying them allows us to enjoy them all year round.

Green skills
Hydrangeas are stunners simply on their own, but I also like to pair mine with cut asparagus fern sitting just underneath them. Beaut!

ASTRANTIA

The deets
One of our all-year-round go-to flowers, each stem is full of at least ten small, pretty star-shaped flowers with the most beautiful pattern. They come in white, burgundy and light pink.

Back to the roots
A genus of herbaceous plants in the family *Apiaceae*, found in central, eastern and southern Europe and across the Caucasus.

Most people assume that the Greek word *astron*, meaning star plays a role in the origin of its name. There are about eight or nine species.

Green skills
This is the perfect filler flower and we use it a lot. Pull it up high to show off all the flowers, or use it lower down within the arrangement, placed next to a lighter colour to provide a beautiful punch of dark burgundy that will guarantee to make the lighter flowers pop.

GREEN BELL

The deets
Ah, green bell, aka Thlaspi, and one my absolute favourites. It is foliage not a flower, and there's a running joke in the shop that whenever I'm checking over someone's arrangement or bouquet, I will always add green bell. I love this delicate foliage, and the way it transforms an arrangement in a really subtle way.

Back to the roots
Thlaspi is a genus of herb hailing from the temperate regions of the Eurasian continent. They are found in central and southern Europe, south-west Asia and two species are native to China.

Green skills
I like making every stem work hard for me, so I cut one stem down into lots of smaller bits and thread them through the arrangement. Or, for a punch of texture, I will use two stems on one side of an arrangement for a bit of that much-desired asymmetry.

FOLIAGE

The deets
Foliage is the glue that binds arrangements together – and what I call the skeleton of your arrangement. There are sooo many varieties. They really bring flowers to life, creating the movement I love to see. In a workshop once, we created an all-foliage arrangement. And boy did they struggle! But going all green can be one of the most elegant, striking and, let's face it, on-trend ways of greening up your gaff. It can also smell amazing.

My top five foliage
- Asparagus fern
- Green bell
- Birch
- Beech
- Eucalyptus

Green skills
Foliage with EVERYTHING! Pull it down, pull it up, create a slice of asymmetry with thicker-leaved foliage through your arrangement.

Flower tools

Even though I love keeping things simple, when it comes to floristry tools I live by the rule 'buy cheap, buy twice'. If you're serious about it, it's worth investing in some serious gear. Luckily, it is relatively easy to get hold of. You can source a lot online, down the market or put it on your Christmas list.

Floral scissors
House scissors just aren't gonna cut it. They will damage the stems and inevitably your display. Invest in a proper pair – Japanese floristry scissors are the best.

Knife
Having good knife skills is useful for stripping tough stems and removing thorns.

Jars
We love a good old jar at G&T. We use jam jars, pickle jars, mayo jars! A great reliable host for your wild flowers!

Twine
To tie the stems of your bouquet together to keep its shape. At Grace & Thorn we just go for the classic, brown and natural.

Kraft paper
Buy some kraft paper and wrap your displays to share the love with your mates and mum.

Stamp and ink
Give your wrapped bouquet a signature sign-off. Search online to make your mark.

Rating
Total diva.

Name check
Looks like a fern, and think 'A' for Aesop.

The deets
The first thing to understand about an asparagus fern is that it is neither a fern nor an asparagus. Instead, it is a climbing plant with lovely big, bushy leaves. There is a beautiful delicacy to the leaves and different types have different textures. The 'Sprengeri', which is really fluffy, is very popular in my shop. It grows really quickly and moults like a motherfucker! Be creative with space. I've trained mine across a window using wire, or else it looks great in hanging baskets. It's really easy to propagate, so buy one and in a few years you may have several.

Back to the roots
It is native to South Africa, meaning it loves bright, indirect sunlight. Watch out for full rays, as the leaves can easily get sunburnt. Give it a good misting to keep up humidity levels. They have learnt to survive during periods of drought, but the leaves can go yellow when thirsty so remember to give it a good drink once a week. When it's growing, feed once a month. Cut everything back in winter, and it loves a good haircut to help it grow big and bushy. Remove any brown leaves when you spot them.

How not to kill your asparagus fern
Because this one is a speedy grower it can quickly outgrow its pot. Once it starts to look too big or you spot roots poking through the bottom, just move it to a bigger pot. When it gets really big, propagate it – take out the roots, divide in half and repot (see page 215).

HOW TO MAKE A HAND-TIED BOUQUET

In almost every traditional floristry handbook you will be presented with the word 'dome' as the benchmark of bouquet perfection. Well, not here. I like to call my shapes 'wild', and to create a bouquet Grace & Thorn-style you're going to have to break some floristry rules.

Going back to bouquet basics, first, we need to learn the twist! This will make your stems spiral, creating your 'wild' structure. From here it's all about creativity, so put your personality into it. Forget perfect, go crazy with colours, height and textures and don't forget to let the flowers breathe!

For your bouquet you'll need a combination of focal flowers, fillers and foliage. Here are some G&T classic combinations:

FOCAL: rose, ranunculus, peony, hydrangea
FILLERS: waxflower, ammi, astrantia, berries
FOLIAGE: asparagus fern, Leucothoe, beech

Prepare each stem by stripping off any leaves that will come below the water in the vase – this is really important, as leaves in the water will rot. Don't be precious, just use your hand to whip them off and scissors to tackle the toughies. Lay your prepared flowers out in front of you so they are easy to access and have your scissors to hand for any strays. Tap shoes on? We're ready to twist.

Step 1.
Take a focal flower in one hand and secure the stem with your thumb. This is your binding point. The closer your thumb is to the flowers, the tighter and smaller your bouquet will be. With your other hand, pick up a filler flower and place the stem across your focal stem at an angle.

Step 2.
Twist the stems around 180 degrees. This can be a bit tricky at first and is ALL about practice. Some of my students hold onto the stems for dear life! Try to loosen your grip so they can move freely. Now you can see the back of your display – no one puts bunchy in a corner!

Step 3.
Repeat step one, adding your next stem from the same direction – you should start to notice the angles that the stems create. As you build your display you want to add foliage to create textures and shape.

Step 4.
1, 2, 3, twist!

Step 5.
As you repeat this process, you will see your spiral form. Now you can start moving the stems up and down to create different heights. It's all about asymmetry. We like to keep our focal plants lower and delicate blooms higher to let them shine.

Step 6.
When you are happy with your display, take a piece of twine and wrap it as close to the binding point as possible. Tie with a simple knot, nothing fancy, and snip off the stems so they are all the same length.

IN A PICKLE

The In a Pickle display is one of Grace & Thorn's signature arrangements. I came up with the concept when I'd just started the business and a friend tasked me with sending something to the head of *The Sunday Times Style* magazine – no biggie! (See page 18 for more on this!) It needed to be something that was a style classic but that would stand out from the crowd. Hence the use of an everyday pickle jar, but with a wild display bursting from it. If you have another small vase or vessel in mind – go for it! As a general rule of thumb though, make the arrangement one-and-a-half times the size of your vessel.

Step 1.
Use foliage at different angles to create your skeleton, with the tallest bit being the top of your arrangement.

Step 2.
Start adding your focal flowers. Don't just place these straight down into the jar but place them at an angle and start to create a natural grid on to which all the other flowers and foliage can sit.

Step 3.
Add your filler. You want to layer the filler and all the smaller interesting bits weaving throughout the focal and foliage, again placing the stems in at different heights and angles.

Step 4.
Keep adding and building up your arrangement by grouping flowers.

Step 5.
Step back make sure you are happy with it all.

Step 6.
Add that extra bit of something different!

6

PLANT PORN

BEGONIA

RATING
Attention seeker.

SIZE M

BACK TO THE ROOTS
From moist, tropical places.

HOME FROM HOME
Anywhere they can be seen and admired.

LET THERE BE LIGHT
Moderate to bright, indirect light is perfect.

DRINK?
Binge drinker – two to three times a week.

HUMIDITY
Lots, please!

TROUBLESOME TRAIT
Their leaves are precious, so only
water the soil.

FERNS

RATING
Handle with care.

SIZE M

BACK TO THE ROOTS
Rainforest floor.

HOME FROM HOME
The humid bathroom.

LET THERE BE LIGHT
Keep it shaded.

DRINK?
Try once a week.

HUMIDITY
They love a spritz now and then.

TROUBLESOME TRAIT
Leaves will turn brown if they get thirsty.

CHEESE PLANT

RATING
Easy as.

SIZE L

BACK TO THE ROOTS
Rainforest climbers.

HOME FROM HOME
Your living room.

LET THERE BE LIGHT
A bright room with a little bit of shade.

DRINK?
Once a week is enough drink for them.

HUMIDITY
Every now and then.

TROUBLESOME TRAIT
Too much water or if it gets too cold
and the leaves will turn yellow.

FIDDLE LEAF FIG

RATING
Handle with care.

SIZE L

BACK TO THE ROOTS
Tropical rainforest.

HOME FROM HOME
The hallway.

LET THERE BE LIGHT
Bright light, indirectly of course.

DRINK?
They're not needy, just once a week is enough.

HUMIDITY
Really likes humidity – mist well.

TROUBLESOME TRAIT
Roots will rot if you leave them in water.

FITTONIA

RATING
Attention seeker.

SIZE M

BACK TO THE ROOTS
Spreads across the rainforest floor.

HOME FROM HOME
Terrarium.

LET THERE BE LIGHT
Nothing too bright.

DRINK?
Loves one.

HUMIDITY
Extra for this guy.

TROUBLESOME TRAIT
If the conditions aren't perfect,
it won't put out.

RUBBER TREE PLANT

RATING
Easy as.

SIZE L

BACK TO THE ROOTS
Regions that are hot and moist.

HOME FROM HOME
Any room it has space to grow.

LET THERE BE LIGHT
Indirect light is its favourite kind, medium to bright.

DRINK?
, Once a week, keep it moist.

HUMIDITY
It'll appreciate a good spritz on
its leaves occasionally.

TROUBLESOME TRAIT
Its leaves will turn yellow if overwatered.

PHILODENDRON

RATING
Easy as.

SIZE L

BACK TO THE ROOTS
Hangs around the rainforest.

HOME FROM HOME
Drape across a wall.

LET THERE BE LIGHT?
Bright but not direct.

DRINK?
Yes, please.

HUMIDITY
Yes, please.

TROUBLESOME TRAIT
It won't hang out in cold spots.

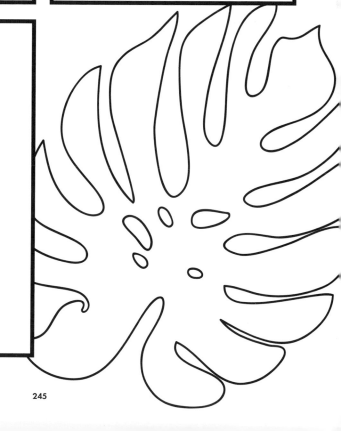

ALOE VERA

RATING
Easy as.

SIZE M

BACK TO THE ROOTS
They are known as the 'Lily of the Desert'.

HOME FROM HOME
A sunny shelf.

LET THERE BE LIGHT
Bright rather than direct light.

DRINK?
Not much; this one's a keeper.

HUMIDITY
No way, that would be too damp.

TROUBLESOME TRAIT
Toxic for cats and dogs.

CACTUS

RATING
Handle with care.

SIZE M

BACK TO THE ROOTS
Desert cacti.

HOME FROM HOME
Your sunniest windowsill.

LET THERE BE LIGHT
Seen much shade in the desert?

DRINK?
Water every other week when the soil is dry.

HUMIDITY
Remember, desert air is dry.

TROUBLESOME TRAIT
Over watering = rot.

BURRO'S TAIL

RATING
Easy as.

SIZE M

BACK TO THE ROOTS
From Mexico, obvs.

HOME FROM HOME
Hanging under a sunny skylight.

LET THERE BE LIGHT
They love bright sunshine.

DRINK?
Can tolerate periods of drought.

HUMIDITY
Nope.

TROUBLESOME TRAIT
If it's thirsty, the leaves will shrivel.

JADE PLANT

RATING
Easy as.

SIZE M

BACK TO THE ROOTS
Africa – not a desert dweller but treat it as one!

HOME FROM HOME
Hot sunny windowsill.

LET THERE BE LIGHT
Full sun please.

DRINK?
They store water in their leaves, so give them a drink once a week.

HUMIDITY
Nah.

TROUBLESOME TRAIT
May become top heavy, so make sure you invest in a heavy pot.

STRING OF HEARTS

RATING
Easy as.

SIZE M

BACK TO THE ROOTS
Discovered hanging from rocks at an altitude of 1,800 feet.

HOME FROM HOME
Spread over a windowsill.

LET THERE BE LIGHT
Full sun for these guys.

DRINK?
Drench the soil but let it dry out before you give it another.

HUMIDITY
Can live with it.

TROUBLESOME TRAIT
Prone to root rot so watch the drink.

SUCCULENTS

RATING
Handle with care.

SIZE S

BACK TO THE ROOTS
Desert dwellers.

HOME FROM HOME
Your desk.

LET THERE BE LIGHT
Loves bright light, but nothing too intense.

DRINK?
Evolved to survive drought so don't over water!

HUMIDITY
Big fat no.

TROUBLESOME TRAIT
There is always a struggling leaf – just snip it off

STRING OF PEARLS

RATING
Handle with care.

SIZE M

BACK TO THE ROOTS
A desert species.

HOME FROM HOME
A sunny shelf to hang out on and from.

LET THERE BE LIGHT
They love a bit of bright light.

DRINK?
Every one to two weeks and less in winter.

HUMIDITY
No way.

TROUBLESOME TRAIT
If it gets cold, the leaves will fall off.

ASPARAGUS FERN

RATING
Handle with care.

SIZE M

BACK TO THE ROOTS
South Africa.

HOME FROM HOME
An east-facing windowsill.

LET THERE BE LIGHT
Can adapt to bright or shady conditions.

DRINK?
Loves one, while the summer's here.

HUMIDITY
Yes, please.

TROUBLESOME TRAIT
Moults like a mother f**er.

CHINESE MONEY PLANT

RATING
Handle with care.

SIZE S

BACK TO THE ROOTS
Native to China (obvs).

HOME FROM HOME
Your desk.

LET THERE BE LIGHT
Not a fan of direct sunlight.

DRINK?
They get thirsty, so keep checking.

HUMIDITY
Tolerant.

TROUBLESOME TRAIT
Their lower leaves droop if they have too much to drink.

BEEFSTEAK

RATING
Handle with care.

SIZE M

BACK TO THE ROOTS
This rare little guy comes from Brazil.

HOME FROM HOME
A nice warm bathroom.

LET THERE BE LIGHT
Start it off in shade but it tolerates more light as it grows.

DRINK?
Yep. Keep it moist.

HUMIDITY
Loves it.

TROUBLESOME TRAIT
No tolerance for cold, dry air.

KENTIA PALM

RATING
Easy as.

SIZE L

BACK TO THE ROOTS
An Aussie.

HOME FROM HOME
Any room you spend a lot of time in, as it is one of the best air purifiers.

LET THERE BE LIGHT
Just not too much as can get sun burn.

DRINK?
Water when the uppermost soil is dry.

HUMIDITY
Yes, please.

TROUBLESOME TRAIT
Can get brown ends due to dry air, so mist, mist, mist.

OXALIS

RATING
Easy as.

SIZE M

BACK TO THE ROOTS
South Africa and South America.

HOME FROM HOME
Shelf saver.

LET THERE BE LIGHT
Not fussy.

DRINK?
Only when the soil on the surface has dried.

HUMIDITY
Don't bother.

TROUBLESOME TRAIT
Need repotting often.

AIR PLANTS

RATING
Easy as.

SIZE S

BACK TO THE ROOTS
Up in the air.

HOME FROM HOME
Anywhere!

LET THERE BE LIGHT
Bright, diffused light.

DRINK?
Mist daily in summer and once or twice a week
in winter. GIve them a bath once a month.

HUMIDITY
Get misting.

TROUBLESOME TRAIT
Direct light will be the death of them.

SPIDER PLANT

RATING
Easy as.

SIZE M

BACK TO THE ROOTS
South Africa, so needs a frost-free home.

HOME FROM HOME
Anywhere!

LET THERE BE LIGHT
Adaptable to both bright light and shade. Clever.

DRINK?
Regularly in the summer time, and a little
less in the winter.

HUMIDITY
Not fussy.

TROUBLESOME TRAIT
Nothing major – just don't over water.

AVOCADO TREE

RATING
Easy as.

SIZE M

BACK TO THE ROOTS
Tropical zones and the Med
with high temperatures.

HOME FROM HOME
A lovely sunny spot with lots of room.

LET THERE BE LIGHT
Give your plant lots of light.

DRINK?
Go on then! Moderate water when the
soil feels dry to touch.

HUMIDITY
Yes. Turn the temp up!

TROUBLESOME TRAIT
You'll have to wait 10 years for a fruit.

LEMON TREE

RATING
Attention seeker.

SIZE M

BACK TO THE ROOTS
Sunny Mediterranean holidays.

HOME FROM HOME
A warm sunny spot. Let them enjoy a summer
holiday outdoors, but bring them in for the winter.

LET THERE BE LIGHT
Yes, lots.

DRINK?
Water well.

HUMIDITY
Spray the soil daily.

TROUBLESOME TRAIT
They hate the cold and you will have to wait a
couple of years for a slice for your G&T.

JASMINE

RATING
Handle with care.

SIZE M

BACK TO THE ROOTS
The Mediterranean.

HOME FROM HOME
On a blooming balcony.

LET THERE BE LIGHT
Bright light with some direct sun.

DRINK?
Plenty.

HUMIDITY
No, keep it fresh.

TROUBLESOME TRAIT
Gets unruly, so prune back.

SCENTED GERANIUMS

RATING
Easy as.

SIZE M

BACK TO THE ROOTS
Hot Mediterranean vibes.

HOME FROM HOME
Bright windowsill.

LET THERE BE LIGHT
Loves lots of sun.

DRINK?
Yes, but always let them dry out.

HUMIDITY
Room temp will do just fine.

TROUBLESOME TRAIT
Will go leggy if they don't get enough light.

TOMATO PLANT

RATING
Easy as.

SIZE M

BACK TO THE ROOTS
Originally South and Central America, but we're more familiar with them from our holidays in the Med.

HOME FROM HOME
Sun, sun, sun.

LET THERE BE LIGHT
Yes, and plenty of it.

DRINK?
Every day, especially when they are growing fruit.

HUMIDITY
Yes, give them a spritz.

TROUBLESOME TRAIT
Rotate them round to keep them straight and tall.

CARNIVOROUS PLANTS

RATING
Attention seeker.

SIZE S

BACK TO THE ROOTS
Wet and humid bog regions.

HOME FROM HOME
Bathroom, with an open window for passing flies to visit.

LET THERE BE LIGHT
Yes, but not direct sunlight.

DRINK?
These plants are always thirsty, but don't give them ordinary tap water as the salts will burn their roots. Use bottled or cooled boiled water.

HUMIDITY
High.

TROUBLESOME TRAIT
They don't like it when you poke your finger in their jaws.

Index A-Z

First published in Great Britain in 2017 by Hodder & Stoughton
An Hachette UK company

1

Copyright © Nik Southern, 2017

A CIP catalogue record for this title is available from the British Library

ISBN 9781473651128

Colour origination by Born Group
Printed and bound by Firmengruppe APPL, aprinta druck, Wemding, Germany

Publisher Briony Gowlett
Project edited by Laura Herring
Design by Laura Liggins
Photography by Oskar Proctor
Illustrations by Jack Bishop
Jacket design by Sarah Christie

Hodder & Stoughton policy is to use papers that are natural, renewable and recyclable products and made from wood grown in sustainable forests. The logging and manufacturing processes are expected to conform to the environmental regulations of the country of origin.

Hodder & Stoughton Ltd
Carmelite House
50 Victoria Embankment
London EC4Y 0DZ

Additional Photography
p13 Geranium © Alexander van Loon/Flickr; https://flic.kr/p/hqF14J; CC BY-SA 2.0
p24 Dinosaur illustration © Look and Learn/Bridgeman Images
p25 Hanging gardens of Babylon © Bettmann/Getty images
p27 Hackney Town Hall © Linda Grove
p28 British floral expert Constance Spry (1886–1960) wraps a bouquet in her flower shop, June 1947 © George Konig/Keystone Features/ Hulton Archive/Getty Images
p29 © B. Taylor/ClassicStock/Topfoto
p46–47 Lamington National Park, rainforest © Jussarian/Flickr; https://flic.kr/p/8KRho; CC BY-SA 2.0
p53 Devil's Ivy and map with Vinny the dog © Bridget Holdsworth/@bridgehfay/jewellery designer @bridgetfaydesigns
p54–55 Garden Canyon © Akos Kokai/Flickr; https://flic.kr/p/pW6wjJ; CC BY 2.0
p64–65 SubTropics © Avalon/Photoshot License/Alamy Stock Photo
p67 Palms © Arturo Garrido/Flickr; https://flic.kr/p/4TVLWi; CC BY 2.0
p72 Geranium plant © Karolina Matykiewicz @marzewiecjestem/Instagram
p73 Jasmine plant © David Q. Cavagnaro/Getty Images
p74 Lemon Tree, Lake Garda, Italy, © Library of Congress's Prints and Photographs division LC-DIG-ppmsc-06475
p76–77 bog image © Haarkon.co.uk
p78 Venus Fly trap © @binchickendeluxe/Instagram
p79 Pitcher plant © Ben Hoeckner @benpossible92/Instagram
p96 Haarkon home office © Haarkon.co.uk
p98–99 Clapton Tram – Photographer: Matt Peberdy www.mattpeberdy.com, Stylist: John Bassam www.JohnBassam.com, Location: Clapton Tram www.ClaptonTram.com
p174 Jardin Majorelle IMG_0677 © Ninara/Flickr; https://flic.kr/p/A46kn; CC BY 2.0
p175 top, left: Jardin Majorelle © Jean Baptiste Bellet/Flickr; https://flic.kr/p/7MX4Xd; CC BY 2.0
p175 top, right: Jardin Majorelle © Scott Wylie/Flickr; https://flic.kr/p/9kqjAv; CC BY 2.0
p175 bottom, left: 20130819_153816 © SnippyHolloW/Flickr; https://flic.kr/p/fFCeb4; CC BY-SA 2.0
p175 bottom, right: La Villa Majorelle © Jean-Pierre Dalbéra/Flickr; https://flic.kr/p/bV19Bh; CC BY 2.0
p182 middle, right: Philodendron Xanadu, © Clutch Chicken
p183 bottom, left: String of Pearls © Italian Supper Club
p188 Pierre Matisse © ARS, NY and DACS, London 2017
p189 © Banco de México Diego Rivera Frida Kahlo Museums Trust, Mexico, D.F./DACS 2017. Image courtesy Leemage/Bridgeman Images
p190 David Hockney *Untitled*, 118", 2010 iPad Drawing © David Hockney
p191 *Still Life with Flowers*, Jacob van Walscapelle (attributed to) 1670-1727 © Rijksmuseum, Amsterdam.

Thanks to my nonna and grandad, for introducing me to the
world of lots of old clutter and plants. Thanks to my family
and my partner, Tom, who believed in me and encouraged me
to follow my passion. Thank you to my friends for all of your
support and giving me jobs where you could! To Katie Harrison
for being just wonderful, to Laura, Oskar and Jack for
their next level design, photos and illustrations that really
brought the book to life. Thanks to the wonderful team at
Hodder: we've laughed (I've cried, hehe) but I am so happy
with the end result. Here's to no more FML feedback!